The Heart

The Heart:

The Living Pump

By Goode P. Davis, Jr., Edwards Park

TORSTAR BOOKS
New York • Toronto

TORSTAR BOOKS INC.
580 White Plains Road
Tarrytown, New York 10591

THE HUMAN BODY
The Heart:
The Living Pump

64667

MAR 2 7 1987

Editor/Publisher
Roy B. Pinchot

Series Editor
Judith Gersten

Volume Editor
Linda S. Glisson

Picture Editor
Leah Bendavid-Val

Book Design
David M. Seager

Art Coordinators
Irwin Glusker, Kristen Reilly

Staff Writers: Wayne Barrett,
Kathy E. Goldberg, Karen Jensen,
Robert D. Selim, Edward O. Welles, Jr.

Director of Text Research: William Rust

Chief Researcher: Bruce A. Lewenstein

Text Researchers
Allison Abood, Susana Barañano,
Heléne Goldberg, E. Cameron Ritchie,
Loraine S. Suskind

Picture Researchers
Jean Shapiro Cantú, Gregory A.
Johnson, Leora Kahn, David Ross,
Johanna Boublik

Technical Illustration Layout
Esperance Shatarah

Art Staff
Raymond J. Ferry, Martha Anne Scheele

Director of Production: Barry Baker

Production Coordinator: Janice Storr

Cover Design: Moonink Communications

Cover Art: Paul Giovanopoulos

In conjunction with this series Torstar Books offers an electronic digital thermometer which provides accurate body temperature readings in large liquid crystal numbers within 60 seconds.
   For more information write to:
   Department F
   Torstar Books Inc.
   580 White Plains Road
   Tarrytown, New York 10591

Authors

Goode P. Davis, Jr., is the author of *Man and Wildlife in Arizona*. He has contributed many articles about ecology to *Defenders Magazine*, and has written a series of articles about the Civil War for the National Park Service.
Edwards Park is senior editor and columnist at *Smithsonian Magazine*. He has shared authorship of many books.

Series Consultants

Donald M. Engelman is Molecular Biophysicist and Biochemist at Yale University and a guest biophysicist at the Brookhaven National Laboratory in New York. A specialist in biological structure, Dr. Engelman has published research in American and European journals. From 1976 to 1980, he was chairman of the Molecular Biology Study Section at the National Institutes of Health.

Stanley Joel Reiser is Professor of Humanities and Technology in Health Care at the University of Texas Health Science Center in Houston. He is the author of *Medicine and the Reign of Technology* and coeditor of *Ethics in Medicine: Historical Perspectives and Contemporary Concerns.*

Harold C. Slavkin, Professor of Biochemistry at USC, directs the Graduate Program in Craniofacial Biology and also serves as Chief of the Laboratory for Developmental Biology in the University's Gerontology Center. His research on the genetic basis of congenital defects of the head and neck has been widely published.

Lewis Thomas is Chancellor of the Memorial Sloan-Kettering Cancer Center in New York City. A member of the National Academy of Sciences, Dr. Thomas has served on advisory councils of the National Institutes of Health. He has written *The Medusa and the Snail* and *The Lives of a Cell*, which received the 1974 National Book Award in Arts and Letters.

Consultants for The Heart

Eugene Braunwald, Hersey Professor of the Theory and Practice of Physic at Harvard Medical School, is Chairman of the Joint Department of Medicine and Physician-in-Chief at Brigham and Beth Israel Hospitals. An authority on cardiovascular disease, Dr. Braunwald has served as advisor to the National Institutes of Health, the National Academy of Sciences, the White House and the World Health Organization. He has recently edited a textbook on heart disease.

John W. Kirklin, Surgeon-in-Chief at the University of Alabama Hospitals, is Fay Fletcher Kerner Professor of Medicine and Chairman of the Department of Surgery at the University of Alabama. A pioneer in open-heart surgery, Dr. Kirklin has won international acclaim for his work in heart valve replacement. A former advisor to the National Institutes of Health, Dr. Kirklin was the 1980 recipient of the Distinguished Service Award from the American Heart Association.

John H. Laragh is Chief of the Cardiology Division, Director of the Cardiovascular Center and Master Professor of Medicine at the New York Hospital-Cornell Medical Center. A consultant to the National Institutes of Health and the editor of a textbook on hypertension, Dr. Laragh is well known for his research in blood pressure physiology and for the recent development of a new technique used in diagnosing and treating hypertension.

Picture Consultants

Amram Cohen is General Surgery Resident at the Walter Reed Army Medical Center in Washington, D.C.

Richard G. Kessel, Professor of Zoology at the University of Iowa, studies cells, tissues and organs with scanning and transmission electron microscopy instruments. He is coauthor of two books on electron microscopy.

Fred Lough is Chief Resident of Thoracic Surgery at the Walter Reed Army Medical Center in Washington, D.C.

© Torstar Books Inc 1984

Library of Congress Cataloging in Publication Data

Davis, Goode P., 1930 –
   The heart, the living pump.

   (The Human body)
   Includes index.
   1. Heart.   2. Heart — Diseases.   I. Park, Edwards.   II. Title.   III. Series
QP111.4.D38   612'.17   81–11269
                                    AACR2

ISBN 0-920269-22-2 (The Human Body series)
ISBN 0-920269-35-4
ISBN 0-920269-36-2 (leatherbound)
ISBN 0-920269-37-0 (school ed.)

20 19 18 17 16 15 14 13 12 11
10   9   8   7   6   5   4   3

Contents

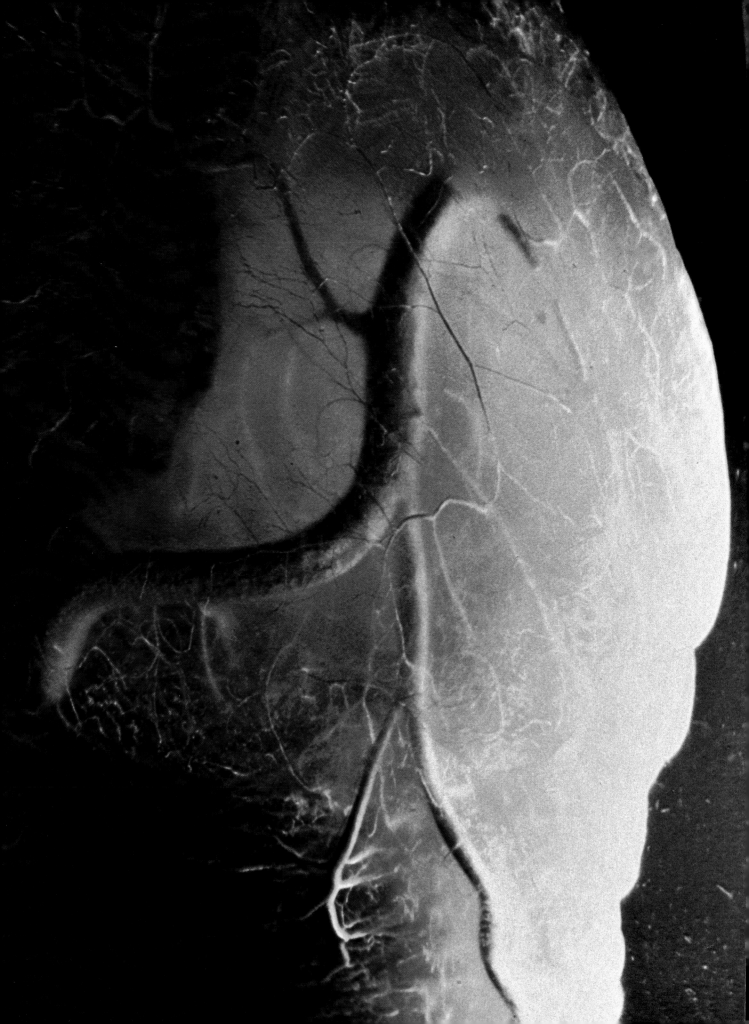

Introduction:

The Sovereign of Life

The heart is a life-giving pump, a simple machine with a sacred mission. Its labor is brute, its fabric coarse, yet the heart connects and sustains the body's work. Cardiac rhythm allows the brain to think, the lungs to breathe and the muscles to move. The heart is the center of life. Seventeenth-century physician William Harvey knew this with certainty. He deemed the heart "the sovereign" of the body.

The heart kindles and keeps life's flame — and so inspires man's awe. In pregnancy's fourth week, a cluster of cells inside the growing embryo suddenly gains purpose. Inexplicably, the cells begin to pulse, sparking a cadence that will carry throughout life. Small wonder, then, that Greek philosopher Aristotle thought the heart the first organ to live and the last to die, an organ from which "the motions of the body commence." To Leonardo da Vinci, lifelong student of anatomy, the heart spoke, if not volumes, then close to it: "With what words will you describe this heart, so as not to fill a book. . . ?"

Heart surgery prior to 1930 was thought akin to medical heresy. Of all the organs, this, the simplest, was the last the scalpel dared touch. Perhaps what kept the heart so long inviolate was man's sense that to cut this organ meant to cut too close to the quick of life. To the ancients, the heart contained the spiritual, not the physiological, essence of man. The Egyptians weighed the hearts of the dead to measure truth while the Greeks saw the heart as a forge, burning impurities from the blood. Centuries later, when the wheel of science turned faster and man learned to move water, he recast this mysterious organ in a new-found image. The heart was a pump.

Today, man knows the heart as a technical masterpiece — and timeless metaphor. From it springs life bound to the virtues of honor, love and courage. The heart ties body to spirit, the mystical past to the practical present.

Embroidered with vessels, the heart circulates the blood. Delicate, durable, this eleven-ounce pump sustains the body's 60,000-mile cardiovascular system. By the heart's power, man lives.

Chapter 1

From Logic to Light

"A merry heart maketh a cheerful countenance," counsels the Book of Proverbs, "but by sorrow of the heart the spirit is broken." In language, hearts not only break, they sing, turn as hard as stone, become heavy or light, cold or warm. Character may be drawn from the pure of heart, the kindhearted, the hale and hearty or the bleeding heart. To speak from the bottom of the heart epitomizes sincerity.

The ancients bequeathed to the ages the romantic, feeling heart — an enduring legacy. But their pragmatic heirs instead devised ways to see and hear the beating heart and to understand more clearly its organic function. They confirmed clinically what their wise predecessors learned from war and athletic games — that the heart cradled the spark of life. A wound to the heart meant almost certain death.

Even man's ancestral relatives, Cro-Magnon cave dwellers, must have suspected that life began and ended with the pulsing, blood-bathed organ inside the chest. From the faded art of a prehistoric painter contemporary man conjectures what Paleolithic hunters knew of the heart's purpose. Working by torchlight, the artist dipped his hand into a basin of red liquid, a solution of iron oxide gleaned from clay. His canvas was a cavern wall in northern Spain. Painting with his fingers, he deftly outlined the profiled figure of an animal he knew well — a mammoth. Below the mammoth's humped back, the artist daubed a mass of color shaped like a heart.

Although his drawing suggests a Stone Age valentine, it may be the earliest known anatomical illustration. Painted about 25,000 years ago, the figure might have shown a hunter where to aim or, perhaps, served as a symbol of the animal's life force. The badge of red marks the spot where a spear thrust surely meant a kill.

Other evidence that prehistoric man may have been aware of the heart's vulnerability exists in

Giants of heart research, "not content to explore with their hands, eyes and ears, began to turn to instruments" like the X-ray and the electrocardiograph. Diego Rivera's mural entitled The History of Cardiological Doctrines *adorns the National Institute of Cardiology in Mexico City.*

Heart-shaped smudge — enhanced in the sketch at left — might have told Stone Age hunters where to aim spears. The drawing, perhaps history's first anatomical record, decorates a Spanish cave.

The pulse could be like "scattered leaves" or "a bubbling spring" to ancient Chinese physicians. They checked arteries from head to foot in diagnosing disease, feeling the left wrist for signals from the heart.

an archaeological relic from Patagonia, a region in southern Argentina. A flint arrowhead penetrating a human breastbone bears witness to a deadly wound of the heart. The dominion of the heart over life and death led certain primitive societies to regard it as the dwelling of the soul. Plagued by evil spirits, the soul was easily lost. Ghosts could steal it by squeezing the heart while a person slept. Sometimes witch doctors were able to coax it back with magic spells.

The Telltale Pulse

"The heart is the root of life," asserts the *Nei Ching*, the collected medical wisdom of Huang Ti, China's legendary Yellow Emperor, said to have lived more than forty-five centuries ago. He believed that the pulse of a healthy heart "flows and connects . . . like a string of red jade." Pulse-taking in ancient China could be an hours-long ceremony. One treatise instructed physicians to take six pulses in the wrists, forearms and hands. Using strong, medium and light pressure, the doctor palpated each point, three times each, for ten minutes at a time. Ten other pulses along the body could also be counted. All were compared with the doctor's own pulses.

To diagnose an illness, the Chinese physician often asked about his patient's dreams. He noted the quality of the patient's voice and determined the keenness of smell and taste. The weather had to be taken into account, and even the time of day. The pulses revealed imbalances between *yin* and *yang*, the feminine and masculine principles embodied in all of nature. Treatment included herbal remedies, acupuncture and blistering the skin with tiny pyres of smoldering mugwort or wormwood. Sometimes a patient was advised to change his ways. Wrong thoughts, he was cautioned, caused lung trouble, but putting bad ideas into practice damaged the heart.

Later, echoing the Chinese, ancient Egyptians considered the heart to be the seat of intelligence and emotion as well as the central organ of life. From the heart, they surmised, stemmed a network of hollow tubes extending to every part of the body. The vessels served as conduits for air, blood, sperm, urine, feces and even tears, all believed to originate in the heart.

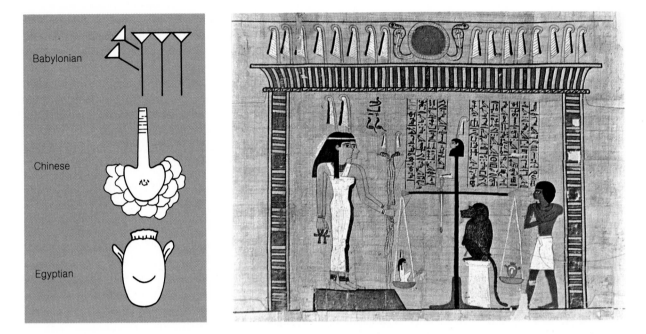

Babylonian

Chinese

Egyptian

Thirty-seven hundred years ago, an Egyptian papyrus recorded that the pulse "measures the heart," enabling the diagnostician "to know what is befalling therein." One of the first to purposely feel a pulse may have been Imhotep, presumed author of a treatise entitled *The Physician's Secret: Knowledge of the Heart's Movement and Knowledge of the Heart.* Imhotep acquired his knowledge during the construction of the Great Pyramids, around 2950 B.C. Perhaps he or some other "physician, priest and Lord of healing" witnessed an accident in which a worker fell and was severely injured. The doctor's observations may have survived on the fragment of papyrus that explains "faintness," a condition in which the "vessels of the heart are dumb, there being no perception of them under thy fingers."

Faint heart and weak pulse told an Egyptian physician his patient was dying. Beyond that, he had scant knowledge of the human body. Forbidden by religious tradition to dissect the dead, the physician brought more scientific skill to the preservation of bodies than to the examination of them. Had they inspected the dead more closely, Egyptian doctors might have discovered atherosclerosis, the blockage of coronary arteries by deposits of fat. The disease has been found in

mummified bodies. Early Egyptians believed that the heart and other major organs had wills of their own and moved around inside the body. Preserving the heart after death was considered necessary to gain immortality. Removed and mummified separately, it was wrapped and placed beside the corpse.

The heart itself remained an object of awe. Egyptians devised hieroglyphs that mirrored its shape — usually a fat vaselike form with handles for the connecting blood vessels. Even older, the Sumerian pictogram for the heart looked like a clam. Later, it evolved into a Babylonian word sign resembling a gate with two trumpets. This symbol represented the heart as home of man's intellect. A scholar of the time would have explained that the heart housed love as well. The cuneiform word suggesting this idea grew from a pictogram of a brazier within a thorax — literally a burning inside the chest.

To the Babylonian physician, a sharp pain in the chest might have signified the presence of demons sent by the gods to inflict disease. He would perform incantations to exorcise the evil spirits or sacrifice an animal in order to divine a cure by reading its liver. He had meager knowledge of the human anatomy and perhaps little

11

A Persian physician takes the pulse of a patient in this illustration from a fifteenth-century manuscript. "A reader of ancient books," he was "experienced in all that healeth and hurteth the body."

incentive to learn. King Hammurabi's Code, written in stone, decreed that a physician whose patient died after an operation should have his hand cut off.

Instead of seeking the help of physicians, early Babylonians often sought the counsel of their peers. According to Greek historian Herodotus, the sick were brought to the marketplace and laid in the street. Passersby stopped before each patient and, "inquiring the nature of his distemper," offered free advice. For good or ill, a patient gained the benefit of accumulated experience, the epitome of folk medicine. As sixteenth-century French essayist Michel de Montaigne once wryly observed, "the whole people was the physician."

In early Greece, the physician was a respected craftsman. The *Odyssey* identifies him as "a wandering stranger . . . one of the itinerant workers for the people . . . welcome the world over." As a "healer of evils," he enjoyed the same social standing as a carpenter or minstrel.

The sixth century B.C. saw the dawning of rational medicine in Greece. Pythagoras founded a school of philosophy that emphasized vegetarian diet, physical exercise, music and meditation. A pupil, Alcmaeon, meditated about the human body and acquired some knowledge of anatomy by dissecting animals. He distinguished the veins from the arteries and concluded that faculties of the mind resided in the brain instead of the heart.

The Father of Medicine, Hippocrates, treated the sick a hundred years later. His name attracted many followers whose collected works compose the *Corpus Hippocraticum*. Of the heart, Hippocratic doctrine speaks uncertainly. Because of its imposing size and compactness, the heart was not deemed susceptible to disease.

The actual workings of the heart remained a mystery to Hippocrates, for man had yet to invent the pump. Thus there could be no understanding that it was the heart's pumping action that caused blood to spurt from a severed artery. Discovering collapsed arteries in corpses may have led the great physician to conclude that the vessels contained only air.

A century later an anonymous contributor to the Hippocratic Collection dissected a mammal's heart. Inside the two major arteries he discovered

"hidden membranes, a structure most worthy of attention." When he poured water into one of the arteries, the membranous valve closed, preventing seepage back into the heart. That, noted the experimenter, was "as it should be," but not because he sensed that the valves affected blood flow. He believed they kept impurities out of the heart, "since the intelligence of man lies in the left cavity." That notion had earlier been rejected by Hippocrates and Plato, both reasoning that man thought with the brain, not the heart. But Plato, visualizing the body as a complex heat generator, theorized that passions originated in the fiery heart.

His independent-thinking pupil, Aristotle, argued that in the heart's moist warmth could be found the "seat of the senses" and the domain of the soul. There too pulsed the soul's vital spirit, which "contracts and expands naturally, and so is able to pull and to thrust from one and the

Hippocrates and Galen speak across centuries in this mosaic from an Italian crypt. One Hippocratic writing states that "from the heart the arteries take their origin and through the vessels the blood is distributed to all the body" — a theory proved by William Harvey twenty centuries later. Galen, surgeon to gladiators, demonstrated that blood alone filled arteries — not air, as Hippocrates concluded.

13

Miguel Servetus

Breath of God, Wrath of Man

"He who really understands what is involved in the breathing of man, has already sensed the breath of God," proclaimed sixteenth-century Spanish theologian and physician Miguel Servetus. Through the study of anatomy, Servetus sought a rational explanation for the Biblical passages placing man's soul in the blood. How, he wondered, did the breath of God reach the blood?

Published in 1553, his last work, the treatise *Christianity Restored*, contains a passage describing the path of blood from the heart to the lungs. Servetus had discovered pulmonary circulation. In doing so, he challenged the wisdom of Galen, second-century Greek physician whose doctrines had survived the Middle Ages to become dogma.

Galen had believed that the blood became a vital spirit by mixing with air in the left ventricle. It flowed from the right side of the heart by way of tiny pores in the midwall. Identifying the vital spirit with the breath of God, Servetus claimed it was produced by another "admirable contrivance." He noted that blood traveled from one side of the heart to the other by way of a "lengthened passage through the lungs, in the course of which it is elaborated and be-

comes of a crimson color." After mixing with air in the lungs, blood became a "fit dwelling-place for the vital spirit," and finally entered the left ventricle of the heart.

But when English physician William Harvey announced his theory of circulation seventy-five years later, he did not know Servetus's work. The Spaniard's contribution was not recognized until almost 1700 when an English surgeon discovered the passage. His theological doctrines declared heresy, Servetus had become a casualty of religious battle.

Servetus lived during the Reformation, a period of religious ferment that led to the division of the Roman Catholic Church and the advent of Protestantism. Rebellious and outspoken, he published his first challenge to church dogma at age twenty. The work

opposed the fundamental doctrine of the Trinity.

The furor aroused by his book forced Servetus to flee his home in Switzerland. Assuming the name of Michel Villanovanus, he moved to France and studied medicine in Paris. After graduating, he became physician to the archbishop of Vienne, but his interest in theology continued to dominate his life.

Hoping to gain the approval of Protestant reformer John Calvin, Servetus sent the theologian a draft of *Christianity Restored*. Outraged by the book's revolutionary ideas, Calvin vowed to have Servetus executed if the Spaniard ever came to Geneva.

Undaunted, Servetus had a thousand copies of the book secretly printed in France. Although he attempted to conceal his identity, the physician was seized and turned over to Catholic authorities. He escaped during the trial but, as if tempting fate, appeared in Geneva a few months later. Calvin ordered him arrested and put on trial for heresy. Found guilty of "infecting" his readers with "unhappy and wretched poison," Servetus was burned at the stake on an October afternoon in 1553, with a copy of the offending book strapped to his waist.

himself had also advised, "If anyone after me becomes like me, fond of work and zealous for truth, let him not conclude hastily from two or three cases, for often he will be enlightened through long experiences, as I have been."

There was no sudden enlightenment in Europe, but elsewhere progress was made. A thirteenth-century Arabian physician, ibn-an-Nafis, theorized that blood flowed from the heart through the lungs and back again. He had read Galen and found errors which he tactfully assigned to scribes. Few people, however, read the corrections of ibn-an-Nafis.

With the dawning of the Renaissance came a renewed quest for knowledge. In Europe's burgeoning universities — Padua, Bologna, Oxford, Cambridge, Paris, Pisa — medical students pushed and probed at Galen's theories. But since church officials continued to oppose human dissection, they could push only so far.

What the Eye Beheld

The study of human anatomy revived through art rather than science. Leonardo da Vinci secretly dissected the human body to learn how to illustrate it more accurately. Overcoming his "fear of living in the night hours in the company of those corpses, quartered and flayed and horrible to see," he deftly stripped away the flesh. An accomplished engineer, he recognized the heart as a four-chambered pump, Galen's theories of circulation notwithstanding. Fascinated by the heart's valves, he drew them in detail. He reasoned that the heart's pumping action, the rush of blood through valves and vessels, generated body heat in the same manner that churning warmed freshly made butter. Blood in the heart must be warm, he said, in order for the "vivifying" process — the bringing of life to the tissues — to work. He described arteriosclerosis, finding that in old men the incessant flow through the vessels made them "thicken and become callous, so that at last they close up and prevent the passage of blood." Despite all he had seen, Leonardo remained a Galenist and a romantic. "The tears come from the heart," he wrote, "not from the brain." He was an observer in the field of anatomy, not a questioner.

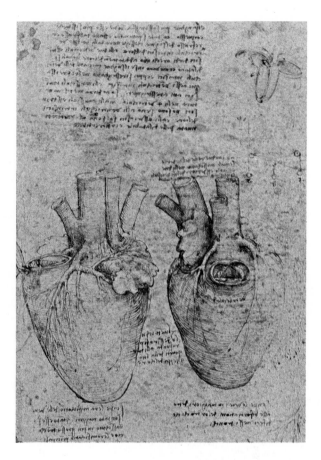

The heart drawn by Leonardo combines science and art. He poured wax down the aorta, then made a glass-lined hollow cast that enabled him "to see in the glass what the blood does in the heart."

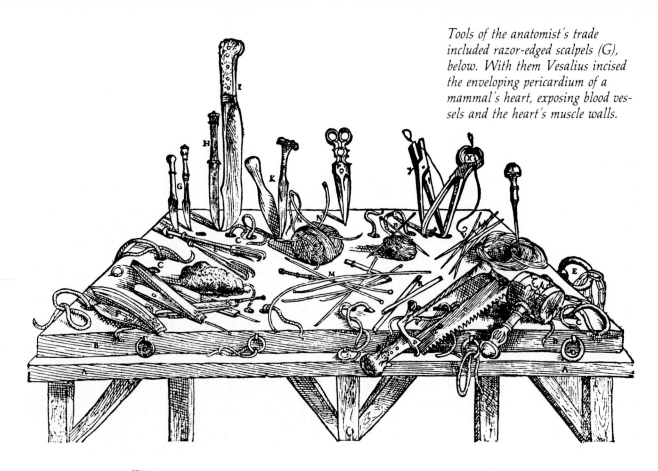

Tools of the anatomist's trade included razor-edged scalpels (G), below. With them Vesalius incised the enveloping pericardium of a mammal's heart, exposing blood vessels and the heart's muscle walls.

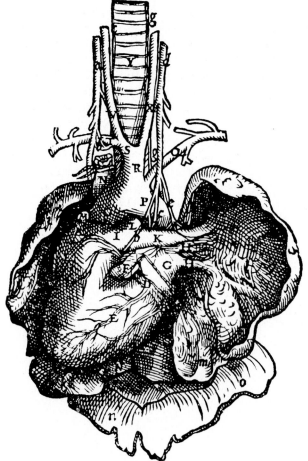

Andreas Vesalius was a questioner. A youth of great curiosity, the Flemish student determined to dissect everything he could lay his hands on. In the early 1500s, he studied in Paris under master anatomist Jacques Dubois, known to all as Sylvius. To his great disillusionment, Vesalius found that "wholly unskilled barbers" performed the dissections while Sylvius stood grandly aside and directed. When the anatomical evidence revealed that Galen had erred, Sylvius airily explained away the inconsistency. "Times have changed," he would sometimes say. Or he would declare, "people are not the same as in Galen's day." Or "that feature is too decomposed to illustrate Galen's point."

Seething with scorn, Vesalius determined to "put my own hand to the business." At night he stole into the paupers' burying ground and smuggled bodies back to his lodgings. There he doused the noxious remains with vinegar to kill the stench and carefully dissected them, exposing one Galenic error after another.

At Padua, Vesalius taught anatomy and began writing *De Humani Corporis Fabrica Libri Septem* — Seven Books About the Structure of the Human Body. The illustrated volumes marked Vesalius as the father of modern anatomy. In describing the heart, he made it clear that there were no mysterious pores in the septum through which blood could seep from one ventricle to another. Yet the headstrong Belgian did not actually say that Galen was wrong, for even he "did not dare to swerve a nail's breadth from the doctrines of the Prince of Medicine." To avoid a clash with the church, Vesalius could only imply his doubts. He marveled "at the handiwork of the Almighty, by means of which the blood sweats from the right into the left ventricle through passages which escape human vision."

Despite his caution, Vesalius ran into trouble. Sylvius pointed an accusing finger at him. Even a former student, Realdus Columbus, railed against him from the Chair of Surgery at Padua, where Vesalius had once reigned supreme.

Hurt and angry, Vesalius burned the manuscripts he had been working on and accepted the post of court physician to Spanish Emperor Charles V. In 1555, however, he brought out a new edition of *Fabrica* in which he more boldly expressed his doubts about Galen's heart theories. "The septum of the heart is as thick, dense and compact as the rest of the heart," he insisted. Therefore, he could "not see how the smallest quantity of blood can be transfused . . . from the right ventricle to the left."

Following his own dictum that he who marries must divorce science, Vesalius took a wife and moved to Spain, a land numbed by superstition and the Inquisition. In Madrid, the anatomist "could not lay his hand on so much as a dried skull, much less have the chance of making a dissection." Vesalius hoped to study once more "that true bible . . . the human body." But it was not to be. He died at age 50 in 1564.

A year later, Hieronymus Fabricius became professor of surgery at Padua. He nearly determined how blood circulates throughout the body. He thought through "little doors of the veins" — the valves — blood was "distributed in a certain just measure and admirable proportion for maintaining the nourishment of the several parts." In 1600, Fabricius, old and weighted with honors, taught anatomy to a young English student destined to fathom the circulation of blood. His name was William Harvey.

William Harvey gleams from stained glass at Mayo Foundation House in Rochester, Minnesota. He was the first to prove how blood circulates, in "a state of ceaseless movement" driven by the heart's pumping action. He described the arteries as "vessels carrying blood from the heart to the body, the veins returning blood from the body to the heart." Harvey served as court physician to Charles I, the bearded observer sitting at the table.

Anton van Leeuwenhoek's micro-
scopes dazzle Queen Catherine of
England. A contemporary, Marcello
Malpighi, discovered microscopic
capillaries that proved Harvey's
theory of blood circulation.

When Harvey received his degree at Padua in 1602, Queen Elizabeth still reigned over England. Shakespeare had produced *Hamlet*, penning the immortal lines:

> Now cracks a noble heart. Good night,
> sweet prince,
> And Flights of angels sing thee
> to thy rest!

Harvey formulated his concept of blood circulation after joining the staff of St. Bartholomew's Hospital in London. He observed how the heart's chambers and valves worked — how the blood always traveled only one way, yet refilled a ventricle as soon as it was empty. He saw that not just some of the blood but all of it passed through the lungs, then returned to the heart. If this was the way pulmonary circulation worked, speculated Harvey, perhaps the greater circulation worked in a similar fashion, with the blood in the arteries somehow finding its way to the veins and then returning to the heart.

After conducting many experiments, Harvey determined that the body contained one fairly constant volume of blood. He was "obliged to conclude that in animals the blood is driven round a circuit with an unceasing, circular sort of movement, that this is an activity or function of

the heart which it carries out by virtue of its pulsation, and that in sum it constitutes the sole reason for that heart's pulsatile movement."

Paintings of Harvey show a short, slender man in the high, ruffled collar of the day. His eyes seem to reveal the weariness of a harried scholar. At first reviled for his "strange theories," Harvey gradually came to be honored. His English colleagues showed their appreciation in rhyme that bears a hint of Elizabethan zest:

> There thy *Observing* Eye first found the Art
> Of all the *Wheels* and *Clock-work* of the *Heart*:
> The *mystick causes* of its *Dark Estate,*
> What Pullies *Close* its *Cells,* and what *Dilate,*
> What secret Engines tune the *Pulse,* whose din
> By *Chimes without, Strikes* how things fare *within.*

As age took its toll, Harvey was forced to turn down the presidency of the Royal College of Physicians. Partially paralyzed from stroke, he died in 1657, his eightieth year. In describing the circulatory system, Harvey had written that the arteries would be engorged and the veins dry *"unless* the blood somehow permeates from the arteries back into the veins." He never saw the capillaries but deduced that they must be there. The development of the microscope would soon reveal the answer to the mystery.

Italian anatomist Marcello Malpighi used the new instrument to observe how "the circulation of the blood is clearly exposed" by the tiny blood vessels linking arteries and veins. Microscopes dominated much seventeenth-century research. Dutch cloth merchant Anton van Leeuwenhoek ground single biconvex lenses that could be focused at close range. He used them to good effect in studying capillary circulation and wrote a paper on the "circulation of the blood in fishes."

Harvey had opened a gate through which new knowledge crowded. Confirming Servetus's forgotten discovery of a century earlier, Cornish doctor Richard Lower noted how the purplish blood brought to the heart by the veins changed to bright crimson after passing through the lungs. Another Cornishman, John Mayow, injected a "nitro-aerial spirit" into venous blood and turned it red. He had almost discovered oxygen. A host of other doctors discovered illnesses relating to the heart. Pulmonary edema, the abnormal gathering of fluid in the lungs, was linked to poor circulation through the heart. Hardening of the arteries was noted. So was anoxia, the lack of oxygen in the blood. Doctors discovered that pain in the arms and shoulders could indicate heart disease and saw a connection between distention of the veins of the neck and swelling of the heart's right side.

A Sound of Drums

Their studies led to the development of new techniques, medicines and diagnostic equipment. England's John Floyer invented a watch that yielded an accurate pulse count for one minute. The year was 1707, long before a second hand would be devised for timepieces. English physiologist Stephen Hales, believing the measurement of blood pressure important in diagnosis, inserted glass tubes into the arteries of animals to see how high the blood would rise.

Tapping the wood to check the amount of wine in one of his father's casks influenced the heart research of Joseph Leopold Auenbrugger, son of an Austrian innkeeper. After studying medicine at the University of Vienna, young Auenbrugger tested his theory by tapping a patient's chest. Realizing that different sounds could reveal much about the body's cavities, he developed the method for use in diagnosis. The tapping of a healthy chest, he wrote, "resembles the stifled sound of a drum covered with a thick woollen cloth or other envelope." He observed that "the whole sternum yields as distinct a sound as the sides of the chest, except in the cardiac region, where it is somewhat duller." In fat people, he discovered, a healthy drumbeat was too dull to discern. He noted that when a heart "yields only a sound like that of a fleshy limb when struck — disease exists in that region." No one paid attention to Auenbrugger's diagnosis by percussion until just before his death. His work was discovered by Jean-Nicolas Corvisart, physician to Napoleon and an excellent diagnostician. From a portrait, Corvisart once deduced that the person had died of heart disease. He was right.

Corvisart translated Auenbrugger's book in 1808. One of the first to make use of the discovery was René Laënnec. In 1816, he tried to test a

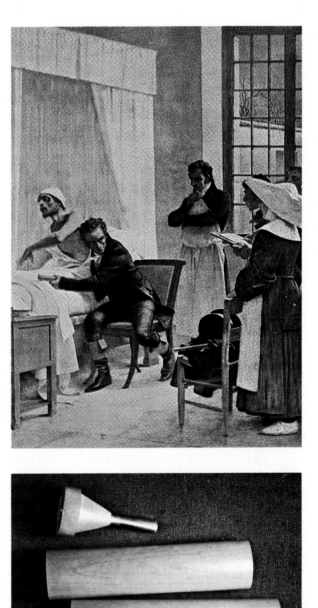

Ear to chest, René Laënnec listens to a patient's heart. With the stethoscope he invented, above, he heard sounds like "a small bell which has just stopped ringing" and "a gnat buzzing within a porcelain vase."

21

fat patient, a girl, and as Auenbrugger had warned, found the percussion too faint. Laënnec usually applied an ancient technique for laying an ear on the patient's chest, but felt in this case it was improper. "I happened to recollect a simple and well-known fact in acoustics," he wrote, "and fancied . . . that it might be turned to some use on the present occasion." Laënnec "rolled a quire of paper into a sort of cylinder and applied one end of it to the region of the heart and the other to my ear." He was "not a little surprised and pleased" to find that he could hear the heart beating more clearly than before. Thus was the stethoscope born. At first a simple tube of wood, it was later made flexible with hollow joints.

Of Foxglove and Poppy

Once he had diagnosed a heart condition, a physician in the late eighteenth century would often prescribe quinine or digitalis. The latter brought fame to English botanist and physician William Withering. From the herb's thimblelike flowers, its digits, came the name digitalis. Withering learned about foxglove's remarkable properties from "Old Mother Hutton," a Shropshire woman who used a potion of herbs to treat dropsy, which caused painful swelling. He singled out foxglove as the active ingredient. Heeding the old wives' tale, Withering boiled or powdered the leaves to extract the essence. He discovered that the drug had "a power over the motion of the heart, to a degree yet unobserved in any other medicine." In 1785, he published *An Account of the Foxglove.* While Withering never understood the full range of the drug's action, he did know that it slowed pulse rate and helped the body rid itself of excess fluid. His "Account" stressed the proper conditions for using the drug, making it clear that it was no panacea.

In 1772, Cambridge-trained William Heberden, dubbed "the last of our learned physicians" by Samuel Johnson, penned a classic description of coronary heart disease. It began as an intense pain in the sternum, or breastbone, often spreading across the chest into the left arm and sometimes the right. Naming the syndrome angina pectoris, he described how the pain usually occurred while the victim was walking uphill and how it often vanished when the patient stood still. After a year or so, noted Heberden, "it will come on not only when the persons are walking, but when they are lying down, especially if they lie on their left side." What treatment did he prescribe? "I have little or nothing to advance," he admitted. Try quiet and warmth, a tot of "spirituous liquors" and opium to help the patient sleep. "I knew one," he said, "who set himself a task of sawing wood for half an hour every day, and was nearly cured."

Heberden's friend, John Fothergill, carried on the study. He noted that an autopsy of a patient who had died "in a sudden and violent transport of anger" revealed evidence of "ossification" — hardening of the arteries. Even Edward Jenner, discoverer of the smallpox vaccine, joined in the search for the causes of angina. He too related angina to hardening of the coronary arteries, those that nourish the heart itself. A few years later, another English doctor, Sir William Osler, suggested a hereditary factor in angina pectoris.

Aneurysm, the ballooning of the walls of the heart or blood vessels, engrossed a number of nineteenth-century physicians, including an American surgeon, Valentine Mott. He tried ligating, or tying off, the affected vessels. Despite initial failure, he ultimately succeeded in ligating more than a hundred aneurysms.

Arteriosclerosis, irregular heartbeat and pericarditis — inflammation of the sac that surrounds the heart — were treated with varying degrees of success. When faced with a knife wound that had pierced the pericardium of a victim, Dominique Larrey, chief surgeon of the French army, at first dressed it with a plaster. The patient promptly tore it off. Larrey then put the man to sleep, carefully made an incision in the pericardium and drained "about a litre of fluid with some blood clot." The operation was a success but there were no medicines to halt inflammation. The patient eventually died.

"Recovery of the patient," pronounced London surgeon George Callender and so documented what may have been the first successful heart surgery. In 1873, he attended a patient who, during a brawl, had been stabbed by a long needle stuck in his coat. Callender chloroformed the

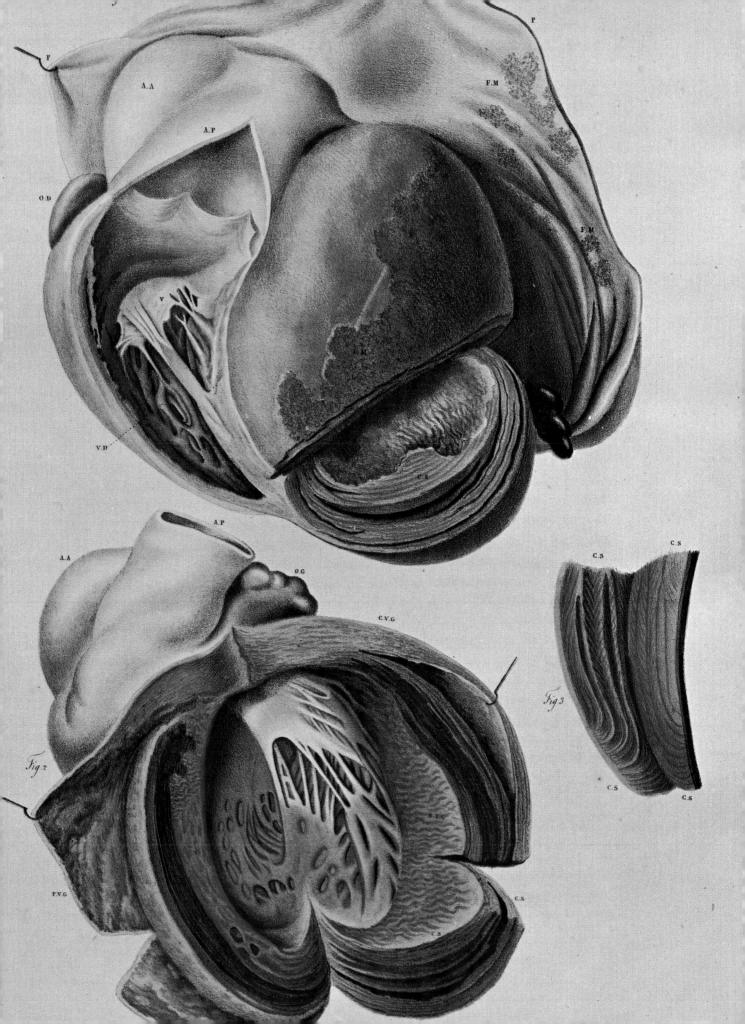

Fig. 2

Fig. 3

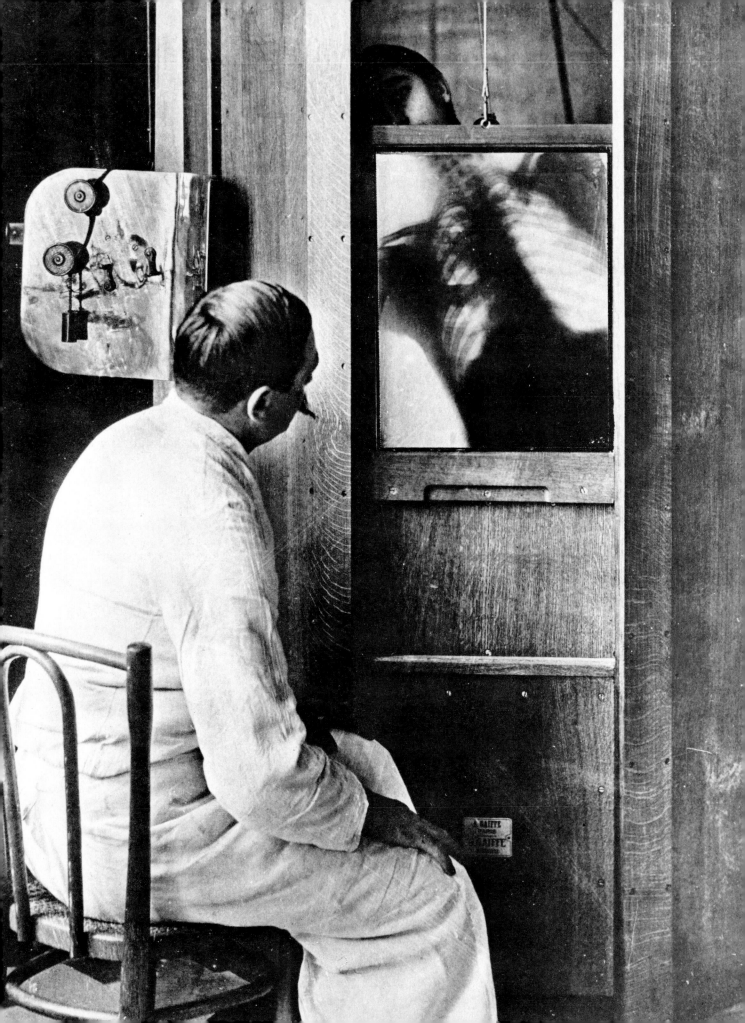

man, then made an incision at a "slight fullness" between two ribs. He found the needle protruding from the heart and making an arc with every beat. Callender plucked out the needle and sewed up his patient. In 1896, Guido Farina tried to save a stabbing victim by suturing the wall of the heart. The patient later died of pneumonia, but an autopsy revealed a perfectly healed heart.

Meanwhile, doctors searching for new diagnostic techniques experimented with devices to measure blood pressure and flow. In 1896, Italian physician Scipioni Riva-Rocci placed a cuff around a patient's upper arm and pumped air into it until the pressure stopped the pulse at the wrist. Slowly releasing the air, he recorded the level of pressure the instant the pulse reappeared. Riva-Rocci's device measured the pressure in the arteries during contraction of the heart. A few years later, Russian physician Nikolai Korotkow placed a stethoscope over the artery at the elbow and listened as air from the cuff was released. He could hear a faint tapping noise, followed by a sharper, louder sound. The former marked the heart in relaxation; the latter signaled its contraction. Korotkow's innovation made possible the modern two-stage reading of blood pressure.

Graphic recordings of pulse rate and rhythm moved from primitive scratches on strips of smoked paper to polygraphic tracings in ink on a long roll of paper. Largely the work of Scottish physician James MacKenzie, this innovation simultaneously recorded heartbeat and the pulses in blood vessels. MacKenzie led a secluded life as a small-town doctor. Through his published writings, his fame spread to other countries. So unrecognized was he in his own country, however, that when German doctors visited London to see him, they were told there was no such man. MacKenzie eventually achieved renown and was made a fellow of the Royal Society.

A Strange Energy Makes Light

Ironically, MacKenzie greeted other new diagnostic tools with skepticism. "When I see the modern cardiologist getting his assistant to take an X-ray photograph of the heart," he wrote, "I am truly amazed . . . that the practice of medicine could have become so futile and ineffective."

The man who discovered X-rays was Wilhelm Roentgen, a German physicist and amateur photographer. In the fall of 1895, while working on the production of iridescent light, Roentgen put a cardboard box over a cathode ray tube, a device used to study the properties of electricity and gases. He turned off the lights and switched on the tube. Although no light escaped from the box, a fluorescent screen near the tube glowed for an instant. Roentgen discovered that the strange energy emanating from the vacuum tube could penetrate books, wood, even flesh. Denser material, like bone, absorbed more rays and left an eerie shadow on the fluorescent screen.

He brought to his laboratory a book containing unexposed photographic plates. He had stuffed the plates — and a metal key — between the pages. Called away in the midst of an experiment, Roentgen laid a glowing vacuum tube on top of the book. Next day, he set out with the book and plates for a session of outdoor photography. He was amazed to find the image of the key on one of the developed pictures. Medicine had gained an incredible new tool. Man could not only see inside himself, he could make a permanent record of what he saw.

Within a year Boston's Francis Henry Williams was demonstrating with the "roentgenoscope" the enlargement of the heart, aneurysms and pericardial bleeding. He had no doubt that X-rays had opened wonderful new opportunities to study the heart. "We may now look," he said, "where we have previously only been able to listen, and sometimes to hear but imperfectly."

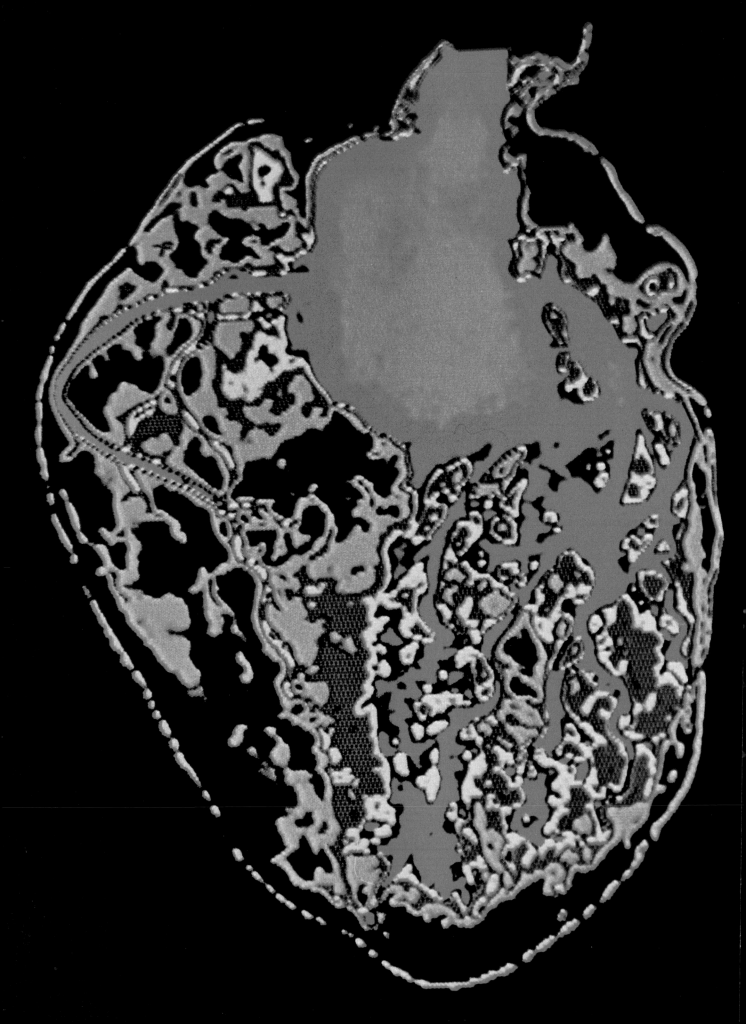

Chapter 2

The Pear-Shaped Heart

Inside the chest, beneath the breastbone lies the human heart. A simple, astonishing organ, the heart is merely a muscle but no less than a fountain of life. In form, the heart is a hollow, pear-shaped bag, separated from top to bottom by a wall of tissue. Each side possesses a small, upper chamber called the atrium, and a larger, lower chamber, the ventricle. Connecting the two chambers, a valve forces blood to flow in only one direction, from the atria to the ventricles and from the ventricles out of the heart. In a healthy heart, no blood passes directly between the left and right halves. As simple as it seems, the heart is the core of life. Author Thomas Thompson described it as "a creature of some internal, unknown majesty."

The importance of the heart to survival can be seen in the speed with which it develops. In the womb the heart evolves in eight weeks from an indistinct clump of cells into the four-chambered form it will carry throughout life. The progress is dynamic. On the forty-eighth day of development, the heart is nine times larger than on day thirty-five. Its cells packed with genetic data rapidly converge and cross, weaving the seamless structure that will one day mean life. Long before any other major organ, the heart and its vessels have taken shape and are ready to function.

The heart begins as two tiny tubes surrounded by a sheath of muscle cells. At the end of the third week after conception, the tubes begin to fuse at the center of the sheath. In a day or two they have joined along the length of their muscular coat to create a single, continuous chamber — a chamber smaller than the period at the end of this sentence. This minute pocket of muscle begins to swell, twist, fold and toughen.

As early as the fourth week of pregnancy, the heart begins to beat. Ebbing and flowing, blood washes through the heart. Chambers form, marked on the outer surface of the organ by shal-

Modern diagnostic tools have given the heart a thousand faces. Its anatomy becomes artistry through the magic of X-rays, computers and video equipment. Physicians can now study bold, revealing likenesses of the human heart and see its beauty and vulnerability in stark detail, as in this image of a massive hemorrhage of the pulmonary trunk, swollen atop the heart.

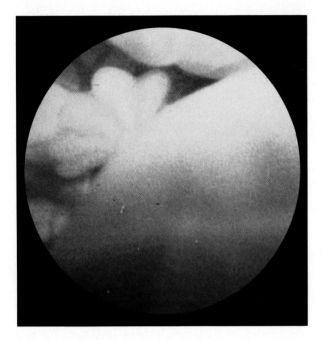

A living fetus, about six weeks old, lies curled in its mother's womb, a budding hand outlined against the placenta, center. Its heart, lower right, appears as a dull red glow beneath its skin.

low grooves called sulci. At the bottom of the heart swells a small cavity with two branches called horns — the sinus venosus. Just above this cavity, the primitive atrium and ventricle appear. A hollow trunk of muscle, the truncus arteriosus, sprouts from the ventricle. A bulging, hollow tube, the heart begins to bend in the middle, doubling over itself into a rough **S**-shape. The heart's furious growth steadily pushes the sinus venosus and the atrium upward and behind the ventricle. The single ventricle splits in two at the center of the **S**, creating new right and left ventricles. As the chambers of the heart take shape, the ebb and flow of blood gives way to one-way circulation. Blood enters the heart through the sinus venosus, flowing in a single stream through the atrium, the left and right ventricles and out the truncus arteriosus.

By the beginning of the second month of development, the squirming embryonic heart has almost assumed the **U**-shape of the adult heart. At the top of the **U**, veins and arteries connect the heart to the embryo's budding circulatory system. The left ventricle lies at the bottom. A partition, the septum primum, gradually emerges in the center of the single atrium and splits it into two chambers. As the atrium divides, the atrioventricular canal, which originally connected the primitive atrium to the left ventricle, shifts to a more central position. Mounds of tissue grow toward each other from the front and back walls, creating two separate canals which connect the separated atria to the ventricles.

Leading from the right ventricle, the truncus arteriosus is, at this point, the only escape route for blood leaving the heart. During the sixth week of development, a thin septum spirals down the center of the truncus and divides it into two blood vessels, the pulmonary artery and the aorta. The full growth of the septum seals off the right ventricle from the left, ending the flow of blood between the two chambers. The left ventricle captures the aortic half of the truncus, gaining its own exit route for blood. While these transformations are occurring, valves begin to form in the pulmonary artery and the aorta, separating them from the heart. Valves also emerge on both sides of the atrioventricular canal.

The tubes soon fuse to form a single chamber. The crude heart swells and begins to beat.

Three weeks after conception of the embryo, the human heart consists of two tiny tubes.

As the primitive atrium takes shape, the heart's tremendous growth drives the atrium upward and behind the dividing ventricles.

Beginning in the fifth week of development, mounds of tissue gradually split the atrioventricular canal into two separate pathways for blood, one through each side of the heart.

Winding down the center of the heart, the spiral septum seals off the right ventricle from the left.

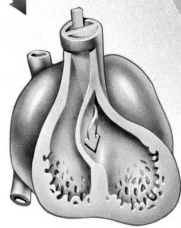

By the end of the eighth week of development, the fetus possesses a tiny replica of the adult heart.

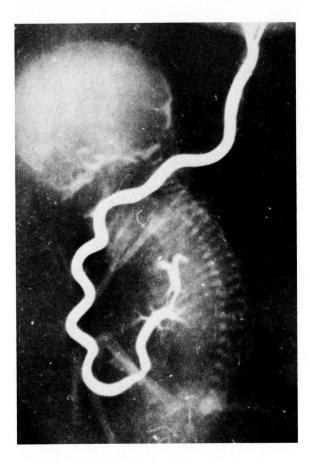 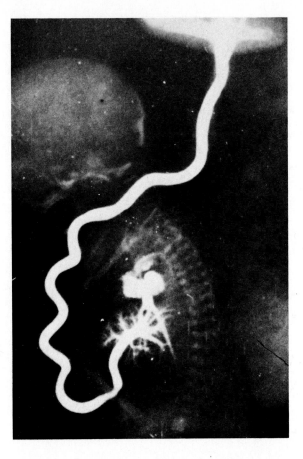

Contrast dye, opaque to X-rays, courses down the umbilical vein of a fourteen-week-old fetus. Bypassing the liver through the ductus venosus, the gleaming white dye flows to the heart, where it divides into two streams, above. Beneath the heart, blood vessels of the liver become visible; above it, a faint trickle of dye creeps up the aorta, above right. Liver and heart glow dully, opposite, as dye flows on to illuminate the aorta and arteries in the neck. A ghostly outline of the brain appears above the heart as the dye in pelvic blood vessels finds umbilical arteries and streams back to the placenta, coiling around the umbilical vein, opposite right, and completing the circuit of life.

By the end of the second month of pregnancy, the heart has distinct right and left ventricles, each with its own major artery. The right horn of the sinus venosus has been incorporated into the right atrium, leaving in its place the superior and inferior venae cavae, the two major blood vessels bringing blood to the heart. Coronary circulation, the flow of blood nourishing the heart's muscle tissue, has also begun. Except for a small hole known as the foramen ovale, two overlapping partitions have separated the right and left atria. Pulmonary veins, bringing blood back from the lungs, now lead into the left atrium. All four of the heart's chambers are distinct. All four heart valves are at work.

Although the fetus's heart has begun to pump blood, its lungs lie sleeping, collapsed. Their responsibility for enriching blood with oxygen will not begin until birth. Tethered to the mother by the umbilical cord, the fetus receives its oxygen-rich blood processed by the mother's lungs.

Blood from the mother flows through the umbilical vein into the inferior vena cava, the large vein in the abdomen of the fetus. Mixing with blood from the trunk and lower limbs, the blood flows up the inferior vena cava into the right atrium of the heart. Some of this blood travels

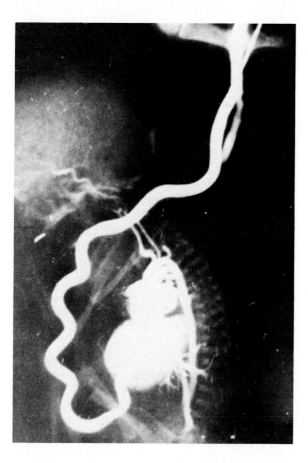
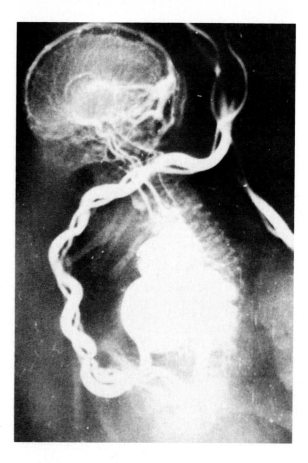

through the foramen ovale into the left atrium. From there it flows into the left ventricle and out the aorta to the body. The remainder drops into the right ventricle, which pumps into the pulmonary artery. But the lungs need only enough blood to grow. Thus most of the blood in the pulmonary artery is siphoned off and fed to the aorta by the ductus arteriosus, a short blood vessel which joins the two major arteries during fetal growth. Blood in the fetus returns to the mother through the umbilical arteries. Soon after birth, the umbilical vein and arteries and the ductus arteriosus wither to become tough ligaments. By the end of the first year of life, the foramen ovale has normally closed, leaving only a shallow, oval scar.

Except for these vital connections between mother and unborn child, the two-month-old fetus possesses a tiny replica of the adult heart. Although no bigger than a pea, this unborn heart is already contracting, already pumping blood, already beating tirelessly in a fetus not yet the size of a man's thumb.

The human heart beats 100,000 times a day, moving more than 2,000 gallons of blood through the body, pumping tens of millions of gallons in a lifetime. Yet when full grown, it is little larger

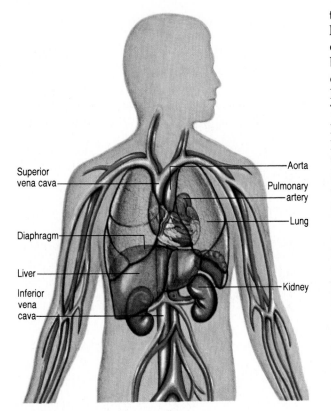

Superior
vena cava

Aorta

Pulmonary
artery

Lung

Diaphragm

Liver

Inferior
vena
cava

Kidney

*Weighing less than a pound, little
larger than a fist, the tireless
heart lies in the center of the chest.
Flanked by the lungs, the heart rests
on the diaphragm, above the liver,
kidneys and other internal organs.
The superior and inferior venae
cavae bring blood to the right
atrium. Atop the heart, the aorta
and pulmonary artery arch upward,
carrying blood from the left and
right ventricles, respectively.*

than a fist and weighs but eleven ounces. Shaped like a blunt, inverted cone, the heart sits slightly off center in the chest, protected front and back by the sternum and spinal column and flanked on both sides by the lungs. Two-thirds of the heart lies to the left of the midline of the chest. The apex of the cone, part of the left ventricle, points downward to the left and rests on the diaphragm. The right and left atria and the origins of the major blood vessels at the top of the heart form the broad base of the inverted cone. In the chest, the right side of the heart projects forward, almost in front of the left.

A shallow channel, the coronary sulcus, encircles the outer surface of the heart, marking the division between the atria and the ventricles. On the front and back of the heart, two other channels called the interventricular sulci designate the boundaries of the right and left ventricles. Blood vessels and fat fill the three major sulci, giving the heart a smooth, rounded contour that enables it to beat vigorously but easily in the surrounding sac known as the pericardium.

Protection and Support

Wrapping the heart from base to tip, the pericardium serves as a protective sheath. Ligaments tether the pericardial sac to the sternum, the spinal column and other parts of the chest cavity, anchoring the heart securely in place. Lining the interior of the pericardium is a thin, moist membrane which climbs from the apex of the heart to the bases of the major blood vessels. There, at a point called the reflection of the pericardium, the membrane folds sharply over, attaches to the outer surface of the heart and descends. Called the epicardium where it descends, the membrane forms the outer layer of the heart wall. A few drops of pericardial fluid fill the space between the two layers of membrane, allowing the heart to beat in a kind of frictionless bath. Inside the epicardium, a thick mass of muscle makes up the bulk of the heart wall. A thin layer of smooth, shiny cells called the endocardium lines the inner surface of the myocardium.

The walls of the heart wrap around a framework of dense, fibrous tissue serving as the skeleton of the heart. This skeleton is composed of

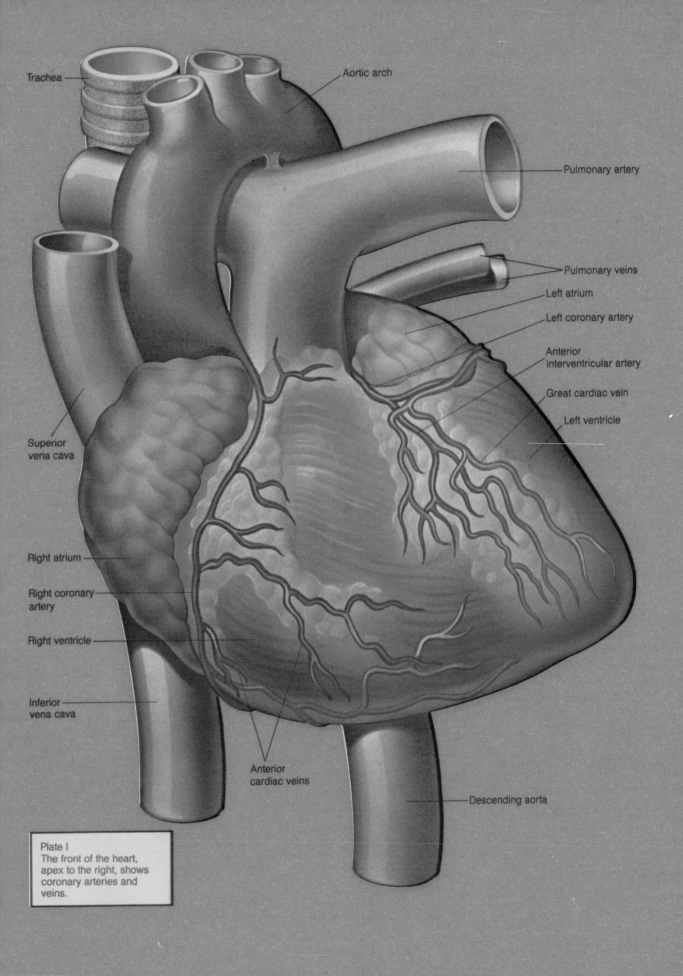

Trachea

Aortic arch

Pulmonary artery

Pulmonary veins

Left atrium

Left coronary artery

Anterior
interventricular artery

Great cardiac vein

Left ventricle

Superior
vena cava

Right atrium

Right coronary
artery

Right ventricle

Inferior
vena cava

Anterior
cardiac veins

Descending aorta

Plate I
The front of the heart,
apex to the right, shows
coronary arteries and
veins.

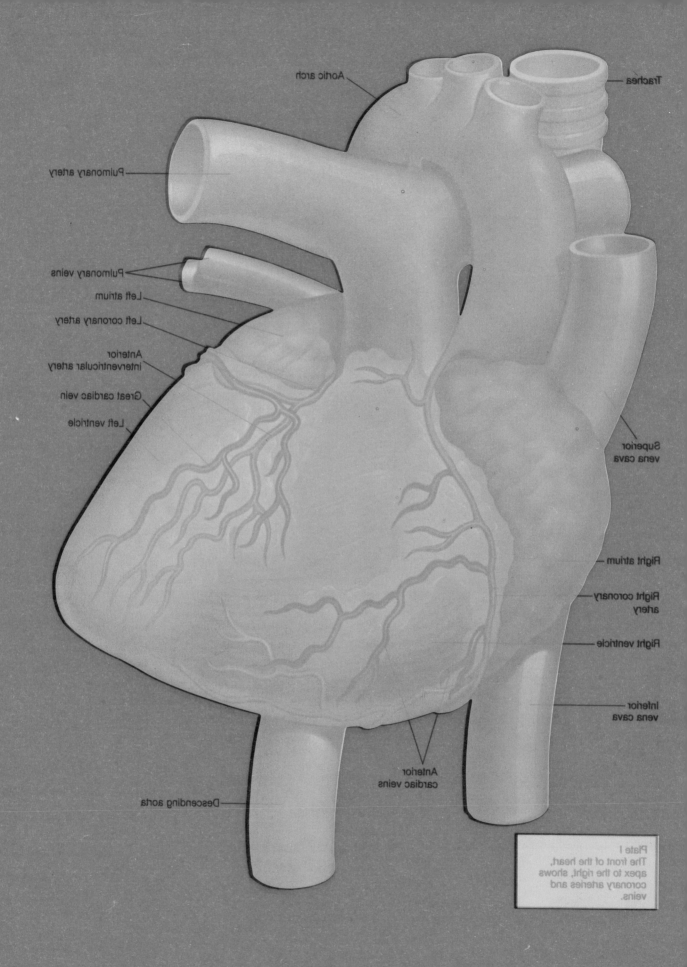

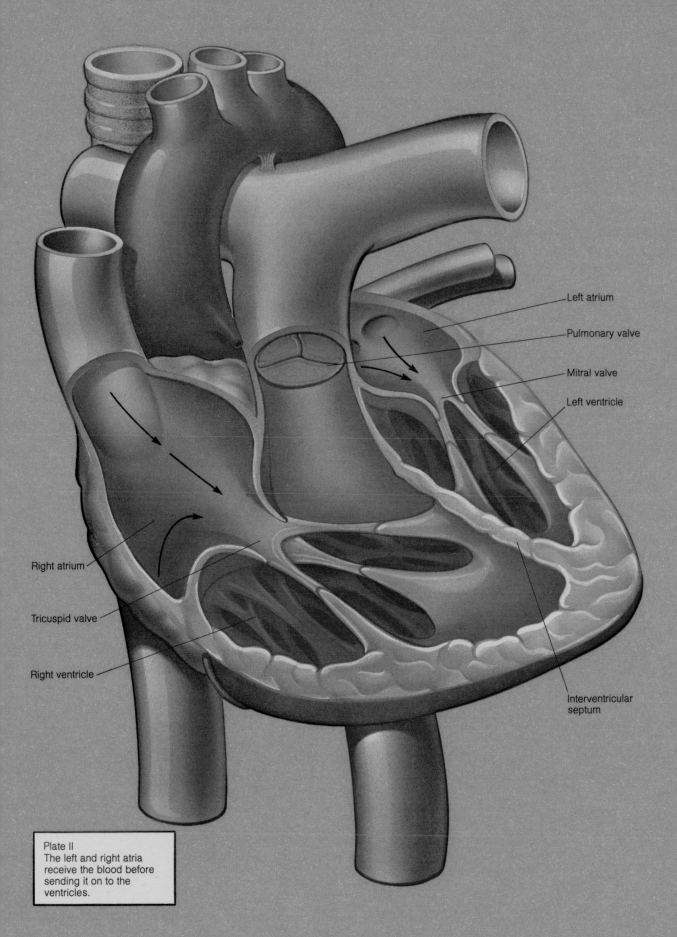

Left atrium

Pulmonary valve

Mitral valve

Left ventricle

Right atrium

Tricuspid valve

Right ventricle

Interventricular septum

Plate II
The left and right atria receive the blood before sending it on to the ventricles.

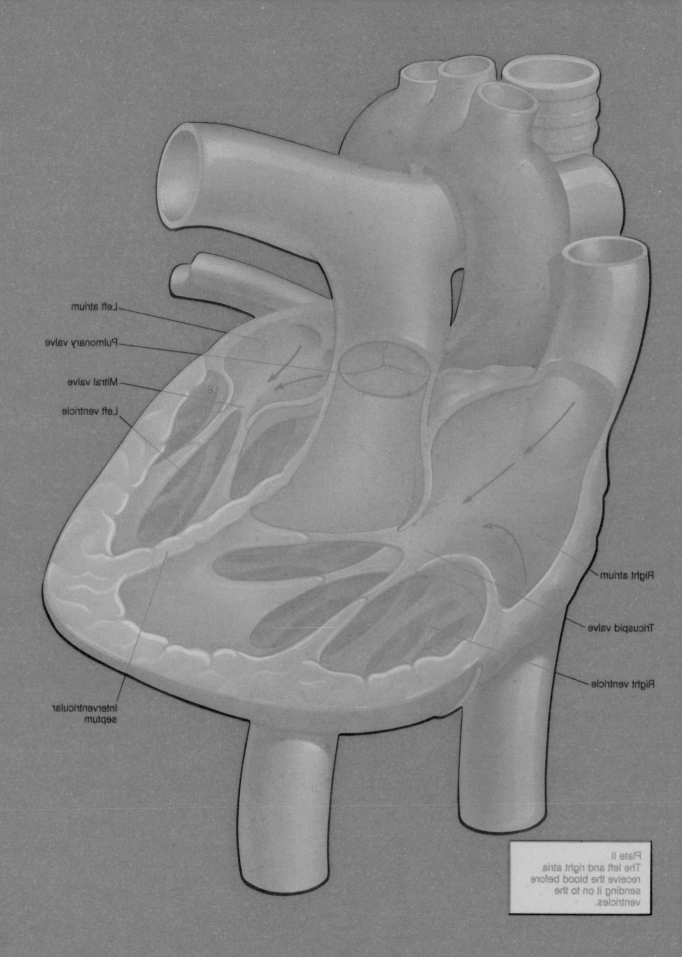

Left atrium

Pulmonary valve

Mitral valve

Left ventricle

Right atrium

Tricuspid valve

Right ventricle

Interventricular septum

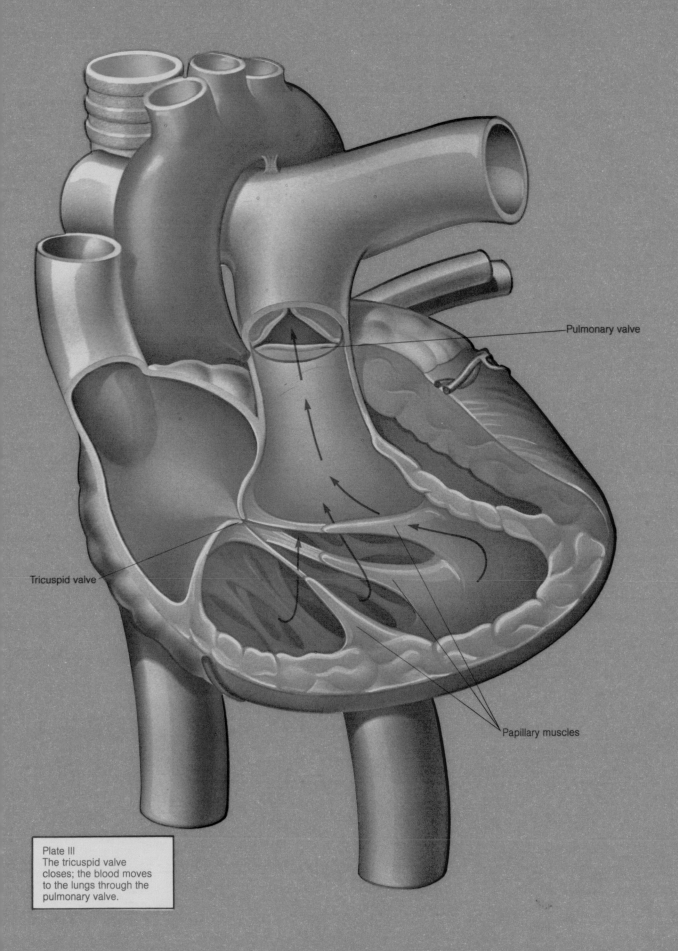

Pulmonary valve

Tricuspid valve

Papillary muscles

Plate III
The tricuspid valve
closes; the blood moves
to the lungs through the
pulmonary valve.

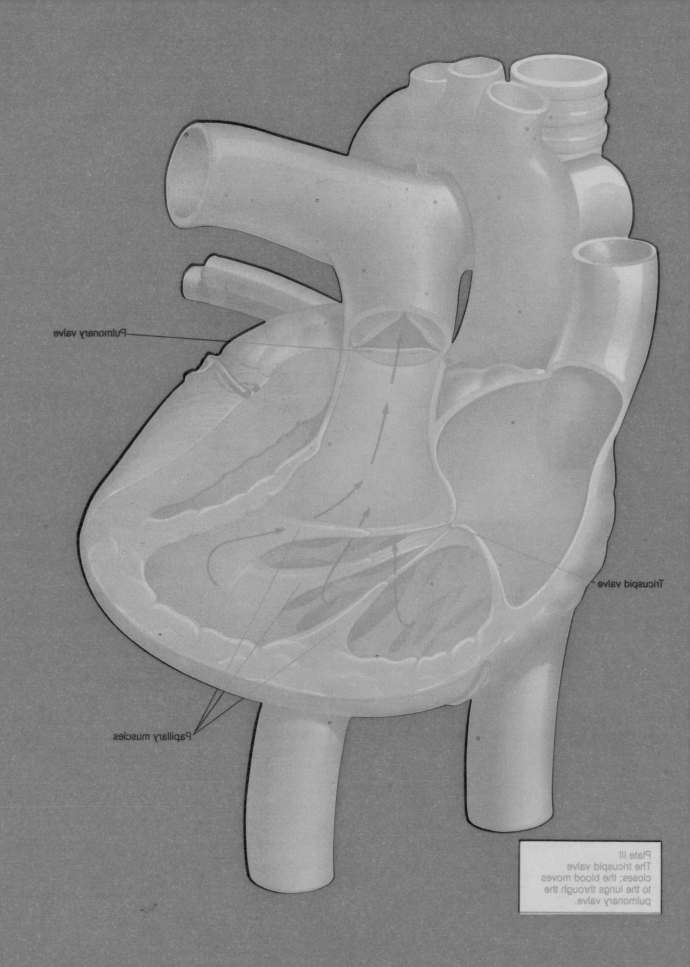

Pulmonary valve

Tricuspid valve

Papillary muscles

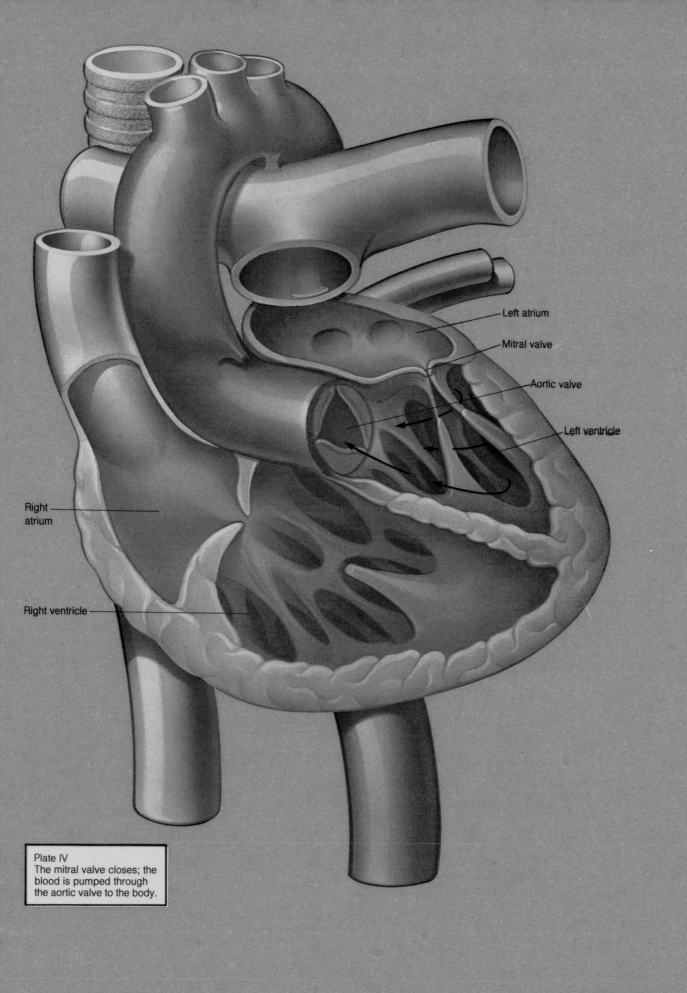

Left atrium

Mitral valve

Aortic valve

Left ventricle

Right
atrium

Right ventricle

Plate IV
The mitral valve closes; the
blood is pumped through
the aortic valve to the body.

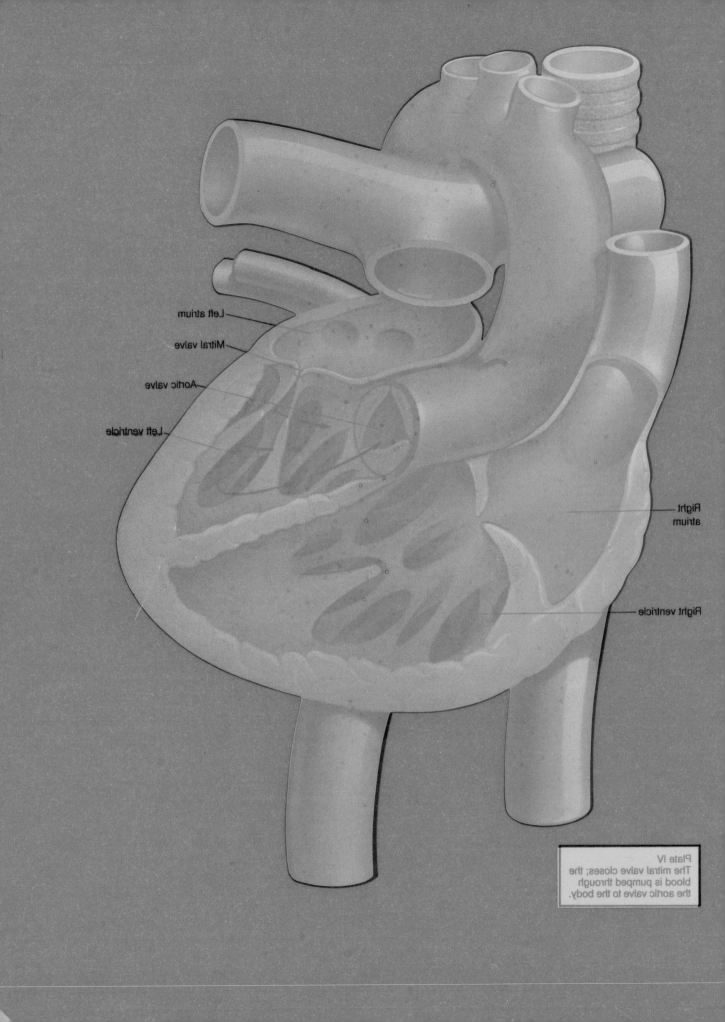

Left atrium

Mitral valve

Aortic valve

Left ventricle

Right
atrium

Right ventricle

Plate IV
The mitral valve closes; the
blood is pumped through
the aortic valve to the body.

A watertight inner lining, a middle layer of muscle and a tough outer sheath form the walls of the hollow heart. Inside the heart, a fibrous skeleton anchors the spiraling bands of muscles, at bottom.

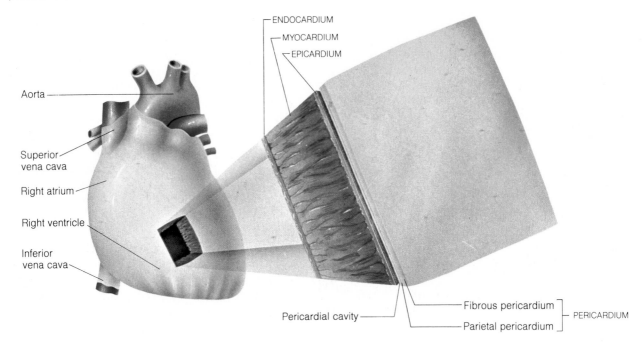

ENDOCARDIUM
MYOCARDIUM
EPICARDIUM

Aorta

Superior vena cava

Right atrium

Right ventricle

Inferior vena cava

Pericardial cavity

Fibrous pericardium ⎤
⎥ PERICARDIUM
Parietal pericardium ⎦

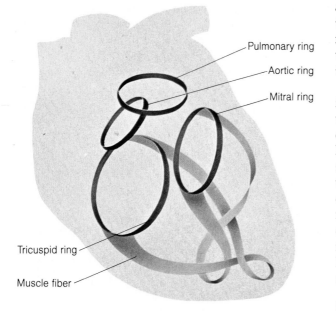

Pulmonary ring
Aortic ring
Mitral ring
Tricuspid ring
Muscle fiber

tough rings around the heart valves, two small triangles called the right and left fibrous trigones and a short, strong cord known as the tendon of the conus. This fiber skeleton holds the heart's muscles firmly in place as they contract. Together with the valves, the skeletal tissue makes up half the heart's weight.

Overlapping layers of muscle, some arching from the skeleton over the atria and back, others winding around the ventricles in rough figure eights, make up the muscular mass of the heart. Each layer is composed of many smaller muscle strands running parallel to each other and wrapped in connective tissue. The strands consist of individual cells of cardiac muscle — the mute, microscopic laborers of the heart. Linked end to end, end to side and side to side in an intricate network, cardiac muscle cells contract with every heartbeat. Their individual efforts merge to create the vital contractions of the heart.

Source of Power

Cardiac muscle differs from muscle fibers in the rest of the body. Skeletal muscle, found in the arms, legs, trunk and head, accounts for much of the body's weight. Also called striated muscle for the stripes that cross the muscle fibers, skeletal

34

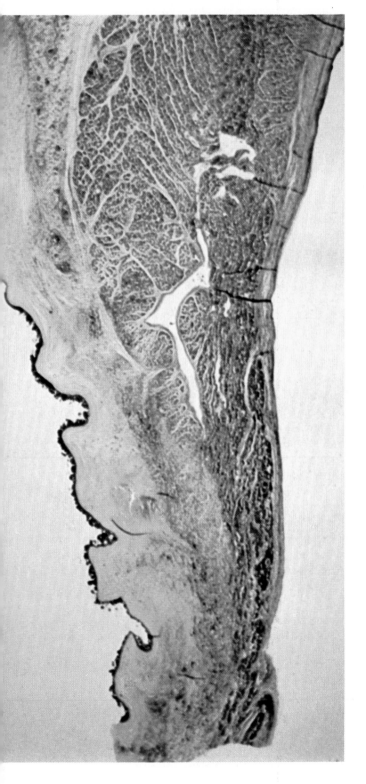

A slice of the heart wall shows the thin, pale epicardium on the left, the broad, dark middle layer of myocardial muscle and the heart's inner lining (the endocardium) only a few cells thick, on the right.

muscle is generally controlled by the voluntary nervous system. Visceral muscle, known as smooth muscle because it lacks stripes, lines the stomach and other internal organs. It responds to the commands of the autonomic, or involuntary, nervous system. But cardiac muscle, as its name suggests, exists only in the heart.

Cardiac muscle fibers possess the striations typical of skeletal muscle, but they obey the instructions of the autonomic nervous system and the heart's own electrical commands. Unlike skeletal muscle fibers, which may have many nuclei, each cardiac fiber has only one nucleus. While skeletal muscle fibers may be inches in length, cardiac fibers are only a few hundredths of an inch long, too small to be seen with the naked eye. Cardiac muscle cells also boast an abundance of mitochondria, the cellular power centers that convert food into energy.

Under the microscope, distinct, dark bands called intercalated disks can be seen where cardiac fibers meet end to end. Although the disks appear thicker and darker than other parts of the cell membrane, like barriers between cardiac fibers, their function is precisely the opposite. At certain points along the intercalated disks, cell membranes of adjoining fibers actually fuse. Two cardiac fibers, in effect, share one membrane at these so-called tight junctions. Electrical current passing through the fibers and signaling them to contract flows almost unimpeded through the tight junctions. At other points along the cell membrane, electrical resistance may be hundreds of times greater. Following the path of least resistance, electricity flows most easily along the length of the fibers. Stimulate one cardiac fiber electrically and, because intercalated disks provide pathways for the message, adjoining fibers will respond. Structurally, the cardiac muscle is a latticework of separate cells. Functionally, it behaves as a syncytium — a group of cells that have merged to act as a single cell.

A series of proteins gives cardiac — and all other — muscle the power to contract. Thin bundles of proteins called myofibrils run the length of each fiber, like small wires embedded in a larger cable. Inside the myofibrils are filaments, tiny threads of protein, arranged in a repeating

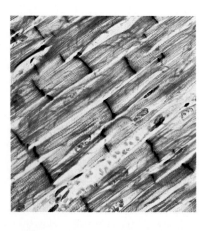

Only cardiac muscle fibers are bound end to end by dark intercalated disks.

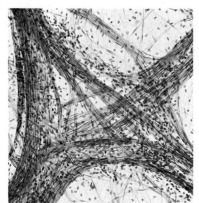

Dark nuclei dot a welter of smooth muscle cells sliced from the human bladder.

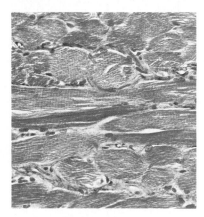

Vertical rows of faintly visible striations label the broad fibers of skeletal muscle.

pattern called a sarcomere. Dark bands across the myofibrils mark the end of one sarcomere and the beginning of the next.

The filaments within each sarcomere are composed of two proteins, actin and myosin. Two clusters of actin molecules, one set in each end of the sarcomere, stretch toward the center but do not quite meet. Continuous threads of myosin, located in the middle of the sarcomere, extend back toward the ends. But they too fall short. The overlapping area, where actin and myosin molecules lie side by side, causes the sarcomere to contract. Tiny hooks on the myosin molecules bind to the actin filaments and pull them toward the center of the sarcomere in a rapid series of ratchetlike movements. When the sarcomeres in a muscle fiber pull together, the fiber contracts, and as its fibers contract, so does the muscle.

The sarcomere in a cardiac fiber must be stretched before it can contract again. Blood flowing into the heart expands the chambers and stretches the muscle walls. As the layers of muscle swell, each sarcomere within them stretches. Within certain physiological limits, the larger the volume of blood that flows into any chamber of the heart, the more powerfully that chamber will contract. First described by Ernest Henry Starling in 1914, this aspect of the heart's behavior is now commonly known as Starling's law of the heart. Partially filled, the atria and ventricles contract weakly; fully stretched, they can push as much as five times the normal volume of blood through the cardiovascular system.

All muscle fibers contract in more or less the same manner. In skeletal and most smooth muscles, the individual fibers contract in response to commands from the central nervous system and from hormones. Instructions from any of these electrical or chemical sources can also affect the heart. But unlike most other muscle cells, cardiac fibers can contract on their own, a potential known as automaticity. At regular intervals, certain special cardiac muscle cells generate their own electrical current, commanding the rest of the heart's fibers to contract. If these special cells fail to generate an impulse on schedule, others take over, producing their own current at slower rates. Some of these special cells are shorter than

Isaac Harary

The Magical Heartbeat

Bending over a microscope in his UCLA laboratory, biochemist Isaac Harary twisted an image into focus. The isolated heart muscle cells under his lens were acting in a way that was surprising but certainly not out of character: the cells were beating.

For centuries, scientists had watched with fascination and puzzlement as disembodied hearts, even when cut into pieces, continued to beat. They searched for hidden nerve endings in heart tissue much as audiences look for concealed springs and wires in a magic act. Shortly before the turn of the twentieth century, scientists learned that the fetal heart began to beat before it had formed any nerve connections at all. They finally concluded that beating arose from an ability of the heart muscle. To unravel the riddle, scientists examined the most basic unit of the heart, its muscle cell.

In a series of experiments conducted in the early 1960s, Harary minced the heart muscle of young rats and then added an enzyme to break down the protein that bonds the cells together. He placed the separated cells in a nutrient medium where they mingled with blood cells and cells of other tissues. Within a few hours, the round heart cells settled to the bottom of the dish, flattened and sent out threads to attach themselves to the bottom of the glass. After achieving the necessary tension, about one in every hundred cells began to beat. The rates of the beating cells — Harary called them leading cells — varied from 10 to 180 beats a minute. Some twitched irregularly; others pulsed like tiny hearts.

The cells began to multiply and soon crowded against one another. As the cells touched, the leading cells imparted their rhythm to following, or nonbeating, cells. And as one throbbing unit met another, they synchronized beats, taking the most rapid rhythm. Steadily pulsing in unison, the heart cells blended into a solid sheet of tissue.

Several years earlier, another scientist had discovered that heart cells of an embryonic chick could beat independently. Harary's experiments with rats proved that the cardiac muscle cells of a mammal retained that ability after birth. His findings suggested that even in mature hearts, the single-minded impulse to beat arises from the heart muscle and that any outside nerve or chemical action is secondary.

Harary speculated that most, if not all, young heart cells had the potential to beat spontaneously. As the heart matures, however, most become the normal, following cells of heart muscle. The highest concentration of leading cells is probably in the heart's pacemaker region. This pacemaker, the sinoatrial node, acts in the fully developed heart much as leading cells did in Harary's lab cultures. It initiates an electric impulse — the ability that had so mystified scientists — to dictate the heart rate. Sparked by the nodes and conducting fibers, the many following cells in heart muscle diligently beat at the rate set by the pacemaker.

But how the cells first begin to contract remains a mystery, a bit of magic waiting to be revealed by a future scientist who, like Harary and others, will ask, "What really makes the heart beat?"

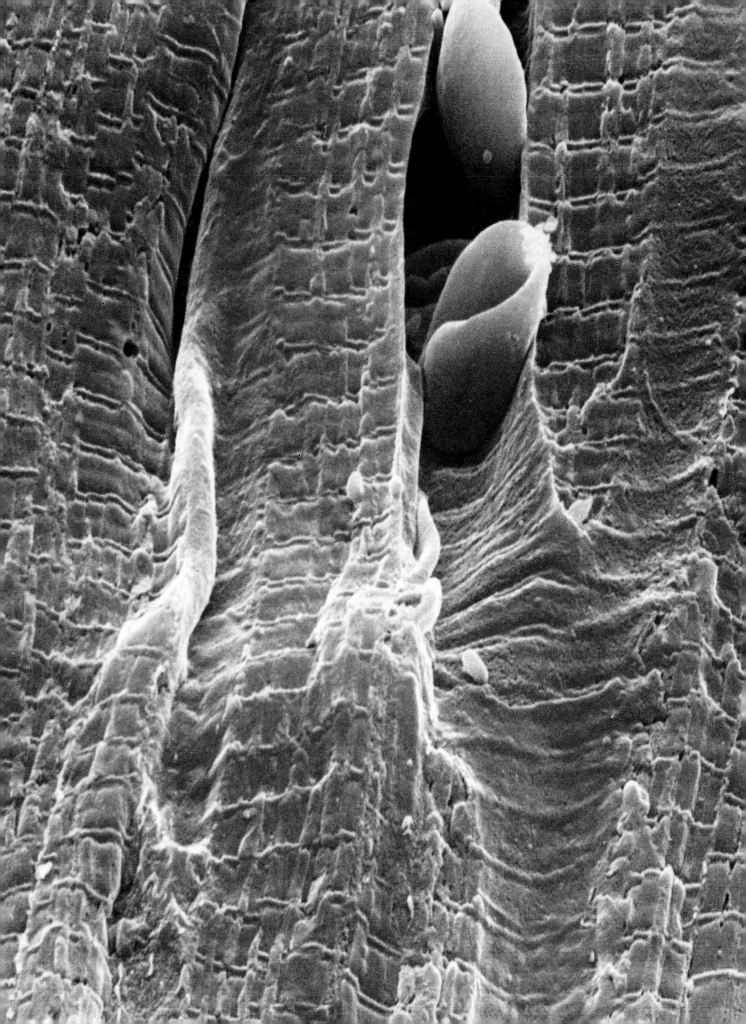

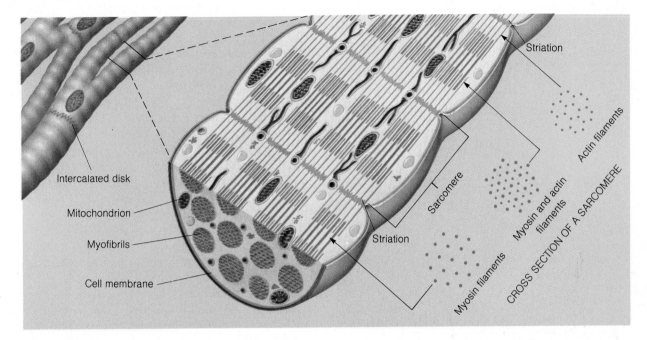

Striation

Actin filaments

Sarcomere

Myosin and actin filaments

CROSS SECTION OF A SARCOMERE

Myosin filaments

Striation

Intercalated disk

Mitochondrion

Myofibrils

Cell membrane

typical cardiac muscle fibers, others narrower, some more oval. Some have fewer myofibrils and less power to contract. But all are muscle cells of the heart, no matter how much they seem to behave like nerve cells. Many scientists have come to believe that all cardiac fibers are, in a sense, both nerve and muscle cells. Cut the heart from the chest and it continues to beat. Cut cells from the heart and under the right circumstances they too will beat. To accomplish their mighty task, the muscles of the heart may possess not only unceasing strength, but also a mind of their own.

Doors of the Heart

Working with the heart's tireless muscles are four heart valves, equally durable, equally essential. Opening and closing with every heartbeat, these valves are one-way doors that control the flow of blood through the heart. Their perfect functioning keeps blood coursing through the body in a fast, endless stream. If damaged or deformed, the valves can disrupt the heart's perfect labor and create a potentially lethal back-up of blood in the veins and arteries, even within the heart itself.

All four of the valves consist of strong, thin cusps of tissue anchored to the tough rings of the

A cardiac muscle fiber reveals its inner workings. Each fiber is composed of myofibrils, bundles of proteins which run roughly parallel down the length of the fiber. Chains of smaller structures called sarcomeres make up each myofibril. Stretching lengthwise inside each sarcomere are overlapping filaments of two proteins, actin and myosin. Contraction and relaxation of the sarcomeres power the beating heart.

Four tissue-thin valves govern the flow of blood through the heart's chambers. Like the heart's other three valves, the pulmonary valve, below, opens and closes roughly once a second for a lifetime.

Stout papillary muscles and inelastic tendons called chordae tendineae rise like the trunk and branches of some subterranean tree, illuminated for an instant in the cavern of the heart's right ventricle.

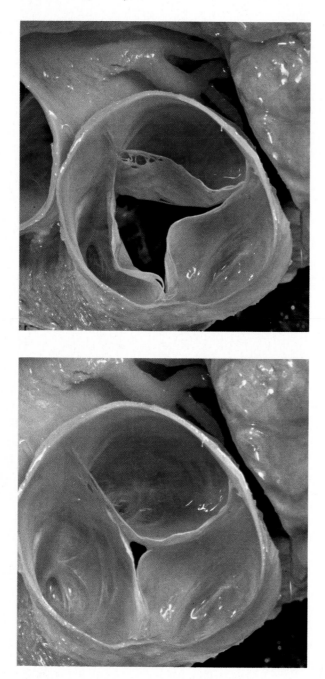

heart's skeleton. The cusps are made of single sheets of fibrous tissue blanketed by folds of endocardial cells. At the base of each valve cusp, the fibrous layer merges with the ring to form a continuous, flexible hinge.

The two atrioventricular valves regulate the flow of blood from the atria into the ventricles. On the right side of the heart is the tricuspid valve, named for its three tooth-shaped cusps. The mitral valve, on the left, resembles a bishop's miter. Both of these valves present a smooth surface to the atria. On the ventricular side, however, inelastic tendons connect the valve flaps to papillary muscles that branch upward from the bottom of the ventricles. When the atria fill with blood, the tricuspid and mitral valves swing open and allow blood to drain into the ventricles. As the ventricles fill and contract, blood presses against the undersides of the valve cusps and forces them together, closing the valves. Simultaneously, the tendons pull on the edges of the cusps to keep them from collapsing back into the atria and impeding the flow of blood.

The blood's only exit from the ventricles is through the semilunar valves, so named for their crescent-shaped cusps. Forced open by pressure in the ventricles, the semilunar valves channel blood into the two major arteries. The valve on the right sends blood coursing into the pulmonary artery. The left semilunar valve directs blood into the aorta. Blood rushing through the valves presses their cusps against the artery walls. When the flow from the heart decreases, blood in the arteries presses down the cusps and pinches their edges together, closing the valves.

The heart's valves, thin membranes that seem almost too fragile for their arduous task, must work constantly. To make an unending stream of blood pumped by the heart, they must open and close more than once a second, every minute, hour after hour, for a lifetime.

Molded together, these valves, tendons, muscles and ligaments form an organ of astounding strength — a kind of hollow, living sculpture as beautiful as it is durable.

The first of the heart's four chambers, the right atrium, receives purplish blood, short of oxygen and laden with carbon dioxide. This used blood

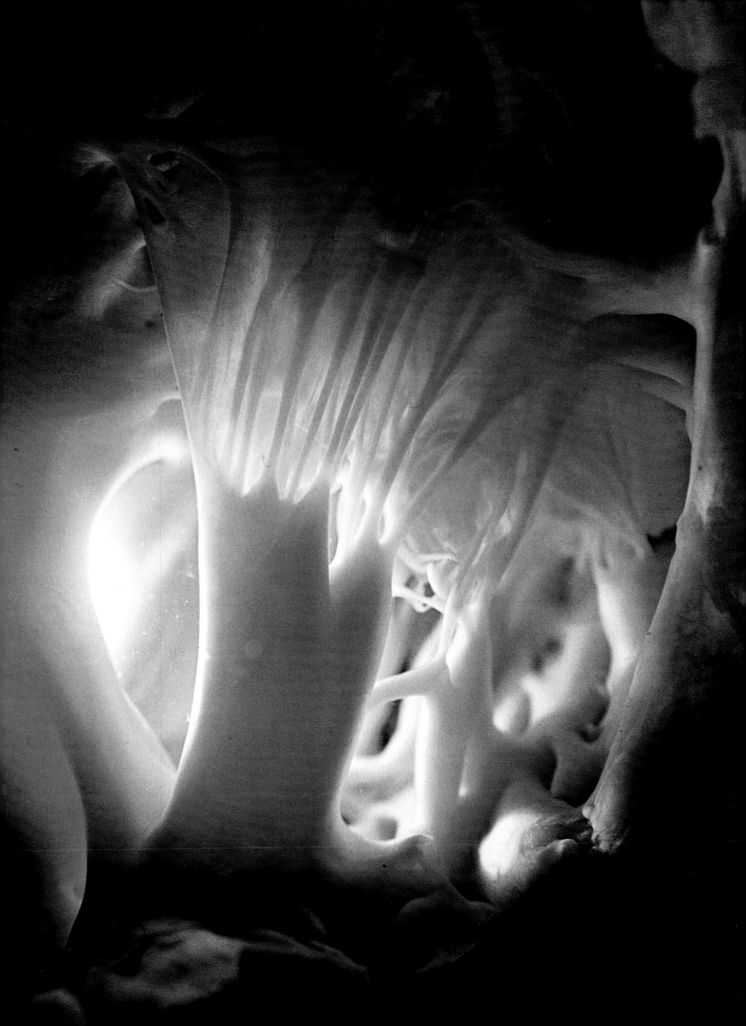

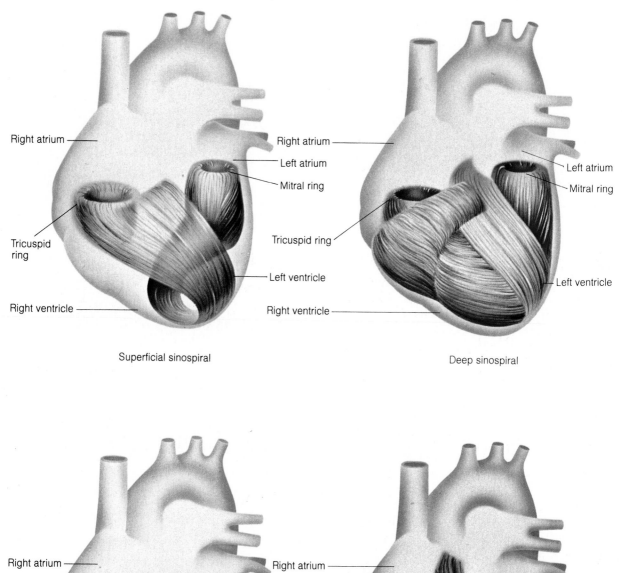

Right atrium

Tricuspid
ring

Right ventricle

Right atrium

Left atrium

Mitral ring

Tricuspid ring

Left ventricle

Right ventricle

Superficial sinospiral

Deep sinospiral

Right atrium

Tricuspid
ring

Right ventricle

Right atrium

Left atrium

Mitral ring

Left ventricle

Right ventricle

Right atrium

Left atrium

Mitral ring

Left ventricle

Superficial bulbo spiral

Deep bulbo spiral

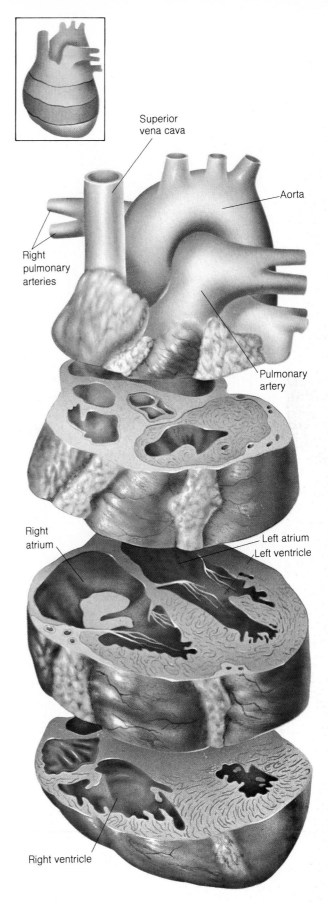

Superior vena cava

Aorta

Right pulmonary arteries

Pulmonary artery

Right atrium

Left atrium

Left ventricle

Right ventricle

arrives through the body's two major veins, the superior and inferior venae cavae, and from the many minute blood vessels that drain blood from the walls of the chamber itself. The atrial walls form a small, smooth dome of muscle with a pouch of folded tissue, the right auricle, perched near the top. Along the inner surface of the auricle, bundles of muscle called musculi pectinati line up in parallel ridges like the teeth of a comb.

The right atrium holds about three-and-a-half tablespoons of blood. Its walls are less than an eighth of an inch thick. Two layers of muscle form the right atrial wall. A superficial layer spans both atria, and an inner layer, composed of many small bundles, arches over the atrial cavity at right angles to the superficial layer.

From the right atrium, the dark, venous blood flows through the tricuspid valve to the right ventricle. A larger, stronger chamber than the atrium, the right ventricle holds slightly more than a quarter cup of blood. Its walls, which are a quarter of an inch thick, are composed of three spiraling layers of muscle: the superficial and deep sinospiral layers and the superficial bulbo spiral layer. All three bands of muscle anchor firmly onto the skeleton of the heart.

Toward the top of the chamber, near the pulmonary artery, the inner surface of the ventricle is smooth. Throughout the rest of the chamber, small bundles of muscle rise from the walls of the ventricle, stretch for fractions of an inch across the chamber, then merge with other bundles. Living threads, they weave an intricate web of tissue across the ventricular wall. Papillary muscles climb up the wall and branch into the short, strong fibers of the chordae tendineae, which anchor the cusps of the tricuspid valve. When the right ventricle contracts, blood rushes into the pulmonary artery and to the lungs.

Four pulmonary veins empty into the main cavity of the left atrium, also a smooth chamber, except for the musculi pectinati inside the left auricle. Although constructed of two overlapping layers of muscle in the same way as the wall of the right atrium, the left atrial wall is slightly thicker and more powerful than its counterpart.

From the left atrium, blood flows through the mitral valve to the left ventricle. This chamber

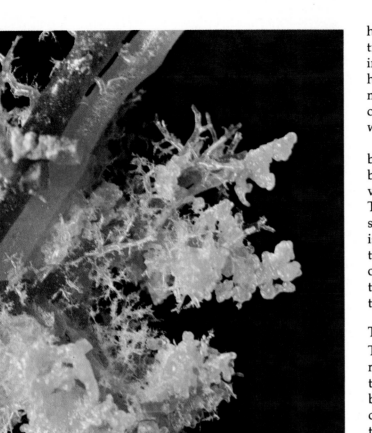

Filling and emptying tiny alveoli, driving red blood cells single file through narrow capillaries, the lungs and heart trade poor air for rich and blue blood for red with every breath and heartbeat.

holds the same volume of blood as the right ventricle, but its walls are three times thicker, making it by far the most powerful chamber in the heart. Its papillary muscles and the cusps of the mitral valve are thicker and stronger than their counterparts on the right side of the heart to withstand higher blood pressure.

Along with the three spiral layers shared by both ventricles, a fourth layer of muscle, the deep bulbo spiral, winds from the aortic and mitral valve rings around the left ventricle and back. This extra layer gives the left ventricle greater strength than any other chamber of the heart. It is strength much needed, because with the contraction of the left ventricle, red blood pushes open the aortic semilunar valve and rushes into the aorta, the first step on its long circuit through the blood vessels of the body.

The Crimson Stream

The path of blood forms a double loop. One route, called systemic circulation, wends its way through all the muscles, organs and tissues of the body, then back to the heart. A second, shorter circuit, the pulmonary circulation, travels only through the lungs. Pulmonary circulation changes blood from a purplish, breathless fluid into a bright crimson stream rich in oxygen.

The pulmonary artery sprouts from the right ventricle and branches into smaller left and right arteries which lead to each lung. Inside the lungs, the arteries divide into smaller and smaller vessels until finally they spread out into a bed of capillaries. Hundreds of miles of these microscopic vessels thread their way through the lungs and wrap around pockets of lung tissue called alveoli. The lungs contain about 750 million of these small air sacs, their combined surface area totaling more than 750 square feet, about the size of a racketball court.

Blood in the capillaries is separated from the air in the alveoli by two thin membranes, each only one cell thick, and by a thin film of fluid. As blood flows through the capillaries, the gases on either side of this infinitesimal divide strain to reach equilibrium. Since the pressure of oxygen in the alveolar air is higher than its pressure in the blood, molecules of oxygen diffuse across the

A wall of tissue only two cells thick, where capillaries cling to alveoli in the lungs, is the site of life's vital exchange between blood and air, oxygen for carbon dioxide. This cast of a corner of the human lung shows veins in blue and clusters of alveoli in yellow. Liquid lucite, stained with different pigments and poured into the lungs and blood vessels of a human cadaver, becomes the clay for this anatomical art. Once the cast has hardened, the tissue has dissolved, creating a colored sculpture of the corridors of the lungs.

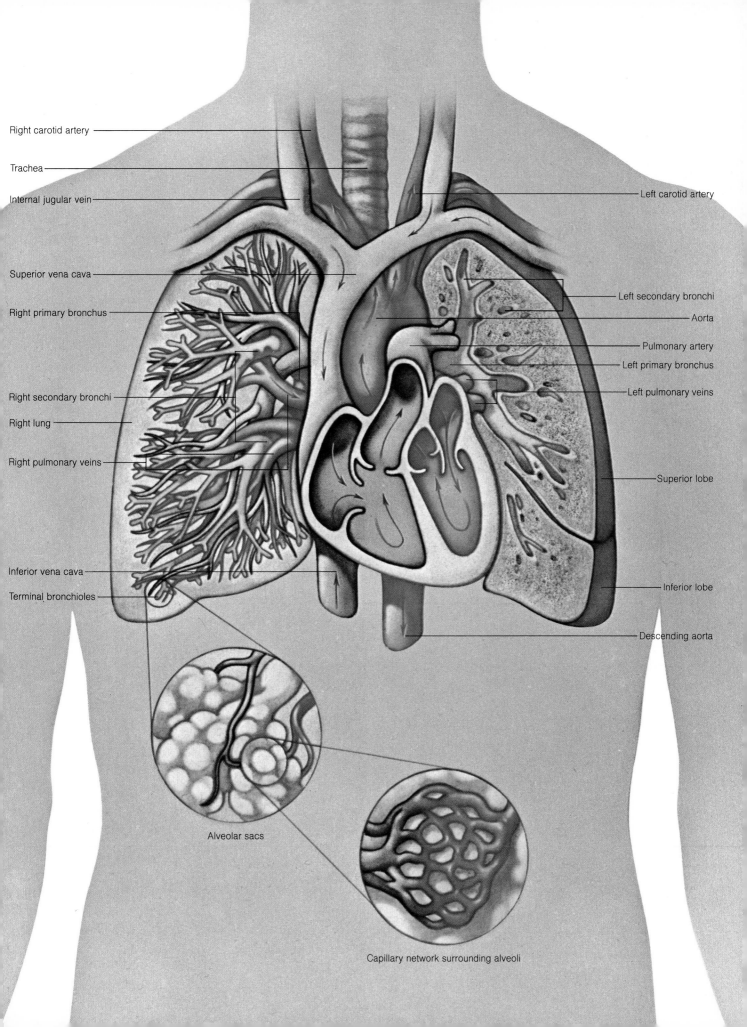

Right carotid artery

Trachea

Internal jugular vein

Left carotid artery

Superior vena cava

Left secondary bronchi

Aorta

Right primary bronchus

Pulmonary artery

Left primary bronchus

Right secondary bronchi

Left pulmonary veins

Right lung

Right pulmonary veins

Superior lobe

Inferior vena cava

Terminal bronchioles

Inferior lobe

Descending aorta

Alveolar sacs

Capillary network surrounding alveoli

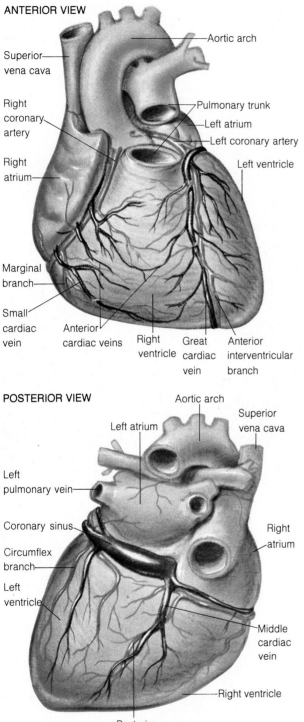

ANTERIOR VIEW

Aortic arch

Superior vena cava

Right coronary artery

Pulmonary trunk

Left atrium

Left coronary artery

Right atrium

Left ventricle

Marginal branch

Small cardiac vein

Anterior cardiac veins

Right ventricle

Great cardiac vein

Anterior interventricular branch

POSTERIOR VIEW

Aortic arch

Left atrium

Superior vena cava

Left pulmonary vein

Coronary sinus

Circumflex branch

Left ventricle

Right atrium

Middle cardiac vein

Right ventricle

Posterior interventricular branch

membranes into the blood. The greater pressure of carbon dioxide in the blood forces the gas to flow from the capillaries into the alveoli.

Blood makes a complete circuit from the right side of the heart through the lungs, back through the left side of the heart and out the aorta every two-and-a-half seconds when a person is at rest. During exercise, the blood can travel this short loop in about one second.

A remarkable blood protein, hemoglobin, is largely responsible for the speed with which this vital exchange occurs. Rich in iron, hemoglobin can unload carbon dioxide and absorb oxygen sixty times faster than blood plasma, the fluid portion of blood. Each molecule of hemoglobin carries four molecules of oxygen to the tissues of the body. It is hemoglobin, when combined with oxygen, that gives blood its bright red color.

Leaving the capillaries, the red blood journeys through progressively larger blood vessels until it flows into one of the four pulmonary veins that empty into the left atrium. From the left atrium, blood flows through the left ventricle and out the aorta to the body. When oxygen-rich blood reaches the tissues of the body, a process much like the transfer of gases in the lungs, but in reverse, occurs. Because the pressure of oxygen in the blood is higher than its pressure in the oxygen-starved cells, molecules of the gas diffuse across the capillary and cell membranes into the cell. Differing pressures move carbon dioxide in the opposite direction. As the blood is drained of oxygen, the molecules of hemoglobin lose their brilliant red stain, leaving the blood a dull purple, the color it wears on its long journey back through the heart to the lungs.

The Internal Crown

To keep the rest of the body supplied with blood, the heart itself must have an ample supply. Only the brain requires more nourishment and oxygen than the heart. This hollow muscle keeps 5 percent of the blood it pumps. Blood is delivered to the tissues of the heart by a system of blood vessels so intricate that every muscle fiber is paralleled by a capillary.

The coronary arteries encircle the broad base of the heart and branch toward the apex like a

46

crown. No larger than a soda straw, the coronary arteries originate just above the aortic valve. In effect, they drain blood from the pockets formed by the cusps of the valves. The left coronary artery divides into the anterior descending artery, which carries blood down the front of the heart to both ventricles, and the circumflex artery, which winds around the back of the heart to nourish the left ventricle and atrium. The right coronary artery curves around the heart, sending one branch, the marginal artery, along the front to bring blood to the right atrium and ventricle. The second branch, the posterior descending artery, travels down the back of the heart, sending smaller arteries to both ventricles. Cardiac veins carry blood back from the muscles of the heart to the coronary sinus, generally paralleling the paths of the major arteries. The coronary sinus drains into the right atrium.

Small branches of the left and right coronary arteries eventually meet in complex junctions known as anastomoses. These junctions can occur anywhere in the body. They can link different branches of the same blood vessel or connect one vessel to another. If a blood clot obstructs one branch of an artery, an anastomosis at the right location can reroute blood around the blocked passage and keep the tissue alive.

The fatal flaw of coronary circulation is a lack of anastomoses between the major arteries of the heart. Many smaller coronary arteries interconnect and can dilate to supply blood to nearby tissue if other blood vessels clog. But a blood clot or an obstructive build-up of fat or cholesterol in one of the main coronary arteries can cut off the flow of blood to crucial areas of heart muscle, sometimes leading to myocardial infarction — literally, heart muscle death — more commonly called a heart attack. The coronary arteries are a crown that keeps the heart alive. Blocked, they prove the king all too mortal.

In a sense the human heart is the epitome of brute labor. No muscle works harder, longer, more steadily. Decade after decade, the heart beats continuously, sometimes for as long as a hundred years. It is, as author John Loughran wrote, "the very essence and poetry of fantastic precision, perfected motion and endurance."

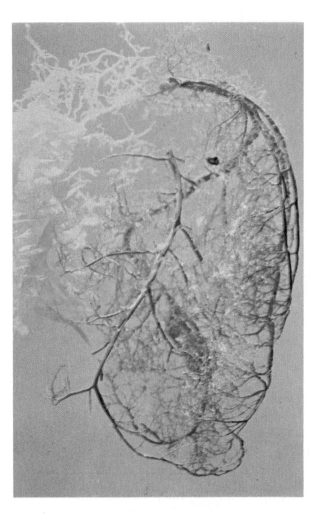

Plastic and acid enable modern anatomists to cast the coronary arteries. Also known as the heart's arterial tree, the coronary arteries fork into increasingly smaller branches, ultimately spreading out into minute capillaries that nourish the tireless muscles of the heart.

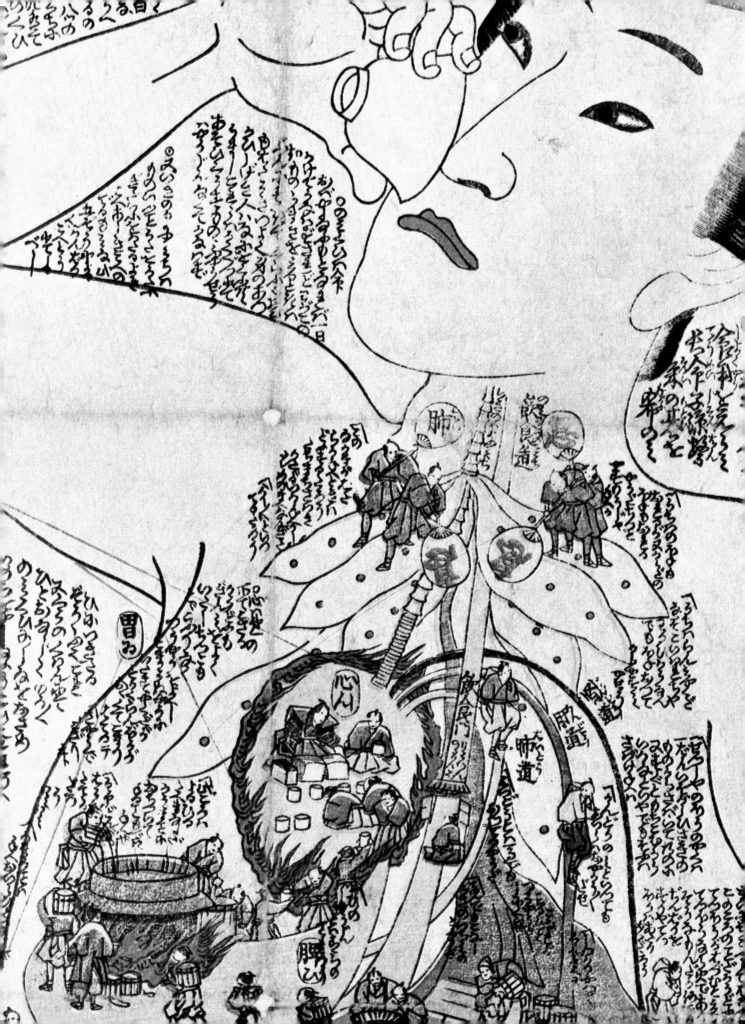

Chapter 3

A Surging Pump

From deep in the chest the rhythm rises, the bass, insistent thud of a beating heart. It is aclean, purposeful sound, one that signals life. With every beat blood washes down through the caverns of the heart, building in mass and pressure, thrusting open first one, then a second pair of valvular floodgates. From there blood surges out through the body's 60,000-mile cardiovascular system to ultimately flood and nourish the deepest reaches of living tissue.

The heart is the power, the center of this miracle. In simplest terms it resembles a pair of pumps, continuously recycling the body's five quarts of blood. But the heart is far more than machine, with its fine, fleshy components pounding, stretching, compressing more than two-and-a-half billion times in a lifetime. Its fiber is not metal that fatigues, nor is its fluid water that in time corrodes. After having served only a few years, manmade valves implanted in a heart often become so worn and pitted that they must be replaced. The heart is sturdier than that. Made of tireless muscle cells, it continually pumps blood — the regenerative material of life. The heart is an engine of hope.

Basic in purpose, intricate in result, the heart feeds the body's every cell. It drives blood into the narrowest capillaries of the vascular system, forcing the exchange of oxygen for the dead weight of carbon dioxide. This it does about seventy times a minute in a healthy, resting adult. At this rate it pumps about 7,500 quarts of blood a day, 680,000 gallons a year. The numbers build so fast they soon lose their power to awe. It is easier to remember the heart's ceaseless beat. Throughout life, from deep in the womb at pregnancy's fourth week until death's final silence, the throb of the heart is always there.

Heartbeat is a simple cadence of contraction and relaxation, known respectively as systole and diastole. This rhythmical power to open and

The "realm of fire" is the heart's domain in this nineteenth-century Japanese print. As recently as a century ago the Japanese based medical practice on lore passed down over generations. At the core of this timeless belief, the heart served as the "lord" of the body.

close derives from the three layers of muscle that wrap the heart. As the layers of muscle contract, they wring the heart of blood. The contraction ripples across the heart in a wave that begins near the top of the right atrium, then crosses both upper chambers. From there the impulse funnels down to the bottom of the heart. The wave of contraction then rises to envelop the ventricles. The heart in contraction simultaneously shortens, flattens and spins about a quarter turn, thrusting the organ's left half out toward the front of the chest.

As both atria relax in diastole they fill with blood. The right atrium takes blood returning from the body via the veins. Purple in hue, it is ladened with carbon dioxide. The left atrium, meanwhile, receives bright red, oxygen-loaded blood from the lungs.

Filled with fluid, the two atria begin the pinch of contraction. They squeeze, increasing pressure on the atrial blood, while below lessened pressure in the relaxed ventricles has already opened the mitral and tricuspid valves. Blood, spilling into the ventricles, pools and rises. Pressure in the lower chambers rapidly grows as the ventricle walls, recoiling from the swelling surge of blood, squeeze into systole. When ventricular pressure

The heart's eternal labor unfolds in the finely tuned rhythm of the cardiac cycle. As the organ relaxes in diastole, both atria simultaneously fill with blood (1). The mitral and tricuspid valves open, and the atria, squeezing into systole, force blood into the ventricles (2). As the fluid collects in the ventricles, they contract, ejecting blood through the semilunar valves to the lungs and body (3). The atria, meanwhile, reenter diastole. They relax and refill with blood (4).

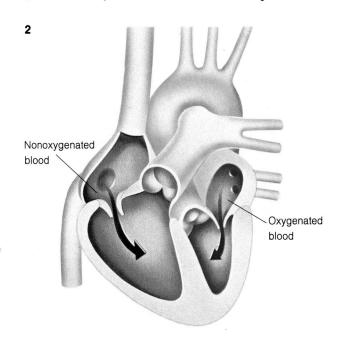

1

Pulmonary valve

Tricuspid valve

Mitral valve

Aortic valve

2

Nonoxygenated blood

Oxygenated blood

exceeds that of the atria, the mitral and tricuspid valves slam shut to prevent blood from flowing back into the atria.

The ventricles are now fully in systole. The pressure of their contraction forces blood upward and thrusts open the semilunar valves, which connect the ventricles to the arteries. The right ventricle ejects used blood into the pulmonary artery, leading to the lungs and oxygen. The left ventricle pumps into the aorta, the huge artery that feeds fresh blood to the body. Pressure in these two arteries rises with the increase in blood volume. When the arterial pressure grows greater than that of the ventricles, the semilunar valves snap shut, locking the blood into its one-way journey. The ventricles, meanwhile, draw a quick diastolic breath as they wait to receive the next batch of blood spilling down from the atria, again caught in systole's gathering grip.

At seventy beats a minute the unbroken round of systole and diastole — the cardiac cycle — lasts about eight-tenths of a second. Within this fragment of time the ventricles are contracting about 40 percent of the time and the atria about 10 percent. Ventricular contraction divides into three uneven segments. A .06 second initial phase yields to a secondary phase of .11 second. In this sixth of a second the ventricle pumps about 60 percent of its blood. It expels the balance in a third phase, also lasting about a sixth of a second.

The heart pieces these fitful mechanical processes into a fine, split-second rhythm through electricity. Where the need for sudden link between body and brain exists, there electrical current flows. Clusters of unique cells lie buried across the field of the heart. These cells can generate their own impulses; they "self-excite." The impulses rip through the heart over pathways designed for rapid conduction, tripping motor response — cardiac contraction — as they go.

Setting the Heart's Tempo

The most important of these self-exciting clusters is a bundle located high in the wall of the right atrium. Called the sinoatrial (SA) node, it serves as the heart's pacemaker. The SA node sets the organ's tempo by kindling the impulses that make it beat. Stimuli from the pacemaker flash across the atrial wall to the septum, the muscle wall dividing the heart's right and left sides. Deep in the septum, close to where the heart's four chambers converge, lies a second group of cells, the atrioventricular (AV) node. This node fields and relays each stimulus down through the

3

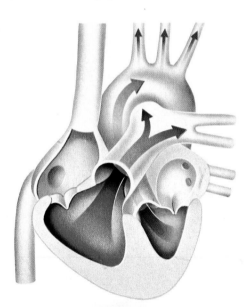

4

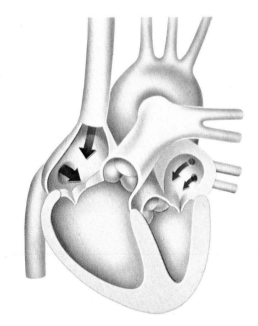

septum to a cluster of fibers between the ventricles, the bundle of His, named for the German physician who discovered it. The bundle of His forks into two branches, each spreading into a profusion of tendrils called the Purkinje fibers. These wire the inner lining of the ventricles, wrapping them in a nerve net that waits for an electrical impulse to galvanize it. When the impulse comes, the heart contracts fully. It must then relax fully before it can contract again. The interval of forced rest, nine times longer in heart than in skeletal muscle, allows the organ to fill with blood. This is called the refractory period.

The magic of the heart's electrical system lies in nature's fundamental drive toward balance. At the hub of this action lies the tiny atom, around whose nucleus circles an arrangement of particles, fixed in their orbit by the forces they exert on each other. Atoms inherently have an equal number of particles that carry a positive charge (protons) and a negative charge (electrons). But it takes energy to hold the particles together, and some atoms tend to lose or gain a particle or two. The elements sodium and potassium often lose an electron, which leaves them with an excess of one proton, or one positive charge. An atom with such an imbalance is said to be "charged." It is called an ion.

In the heart, the cell membrane acts as a pump. It pumps sodium ions out and potassium ions into the cardiac muscle cells. The membrane pumps sodium at a faster rate than potassium. Some potassium ions also leak out of the cell. A relative excess of positive charge soon accumulates outside the cell. Suddenly, after sufficient build-up, the flow inexplicably reverses. Gates in the cell membrane open and sodium gushes back into the cell. This rapid shift creates an electrical current which causes the cell to contract.

Traveling at about two feet a second, this current races from the SA node down a highly conductive nervous path to the AV node, the electrical entrance to the ventricles. There it suddenly slows, moving only two inches per second. At the bundle of His, the current again speeds up. Fanning out through the Purkinje fibers, the signals travel faster than anywhere else in the heart — nearly seven feet per second. The rapid

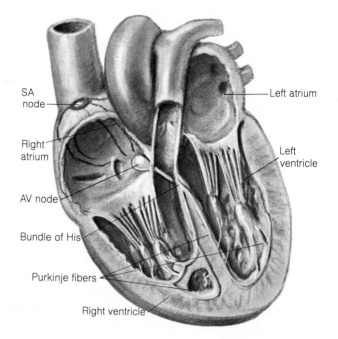

SA node
Right atrium
AV node
Bundle of His
Purkinje fibers
Right ventricle
Left atrium
Left ventricle

Heart's path of fire leads from a special knot of cells called the SA node. It generates electrical stimuli which race down through the heart, sparking contraction as they go. From this cardiac "pacemaker," impulses flash to the AV node and bundle of His before fanning out across the Purkinje fibers which flourish in the ventricles. Fitted together like pieces of a jigsaw puzzle, opposite, Purkinje fiber cells connect via highly conductile intercalated disks, structures that speed impulses through the fibers four times faster than in other areas of heart muscle.

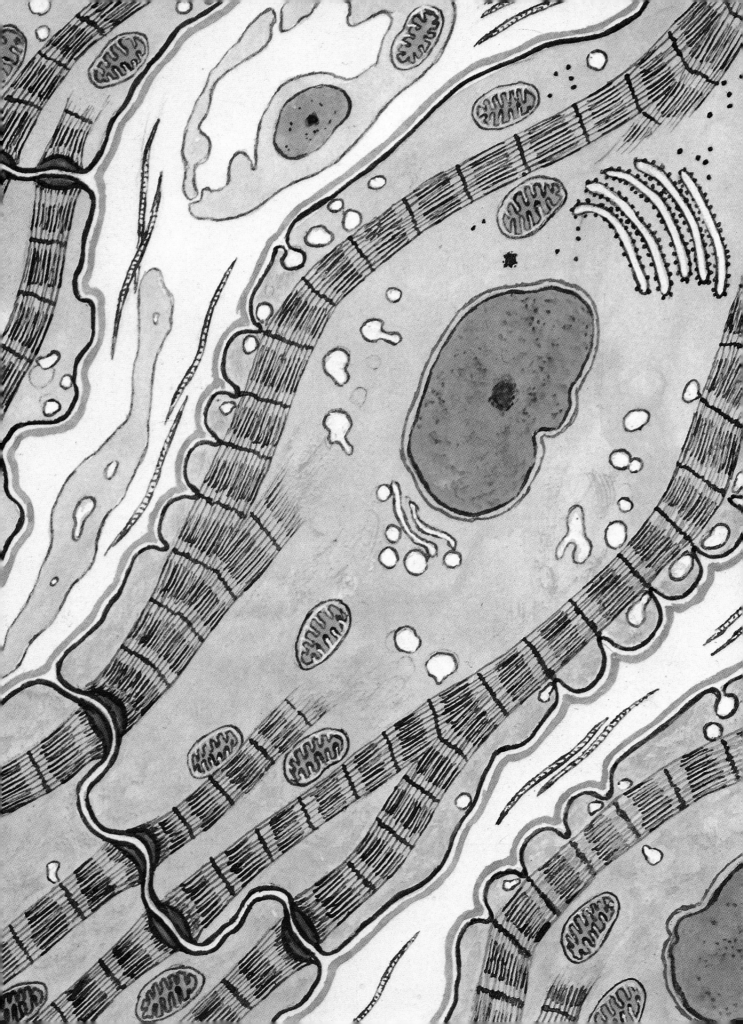

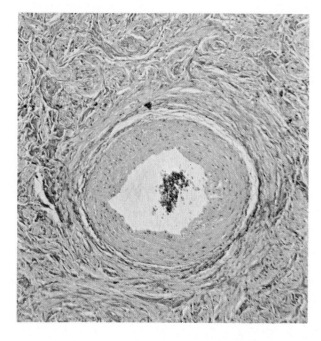

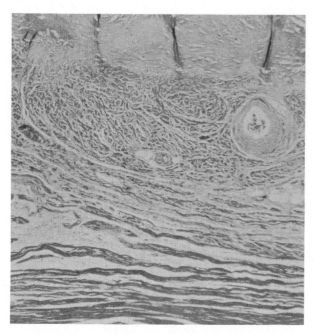

Specialized patches of muscle speed impulses through the heart. Below left, SA nodal fibers fuse with surrounding atrial muscle. Below right, strands of nerve fiber richly layer the AV node.

delivery of impulses by the Purkinje system ensures that the ventricles will contract smoothly.

The sudden reversal of ionic flow through the cell membrane is called depolarization. It quickly yields to repolarization, the pumping of sodium ions back out of the cell and another build-up of positive charge outside the cell wall. Each of these actions causes, and signals, a larger event in the heart. Depolarization accompanies systole; repolarization marks diastole.

Depolarization begins in the cells of the SA node, which has an inherent beat of about seventy times a minute. Seventy separate tidal shifts of ions flow through the cell membrane. The AV node and the Purkinje fibers will also depolarize on their own but at slower rates than the SA node. Since heart-cell contraction is "all or nothing," the other nodes graft their slower rates — about fifty and thirty beats a minute, respectively — onto that of the SA node. If the pacemaker were to stop depolarizing, the AV node would start the beat. If the AV node also failed, the bundle of His would begin the impulse, and if it too stopped, the Purkinje fibers would pinch-hit. Even if all the bundles failed, somewhere deep in the wall of the ventricles a random group of cells would start the beat. They would beat perhaps ten or fifteen times a minute. The slow beat would not be rapid enough to sustain life, but it might serve long enough for emergency medical procedures to restart the pacemaker.

Nature's Fire

That electricity could spring from a biological source was an idea that arose late in the eighteenth century. First evidence surfaced around 1790 in the University of Bologna laboratory of Italian anatomist Luigi Galvani. There, by accident, one of Galvani's assistants touched his scalpel to the leg of a frog lying near a friction machine. The limb jumped.

The friction machine used by Galvani was perhaps the first tangible reward to arise from man's experiments with electrical phenomena. Developed in the 1600s by Prussian scientist Otto von Guericke, the machine consisted of a rotating sulfur globe that became highly charged when rubbed against the hand. In 1745, the Dutch physicist, Cunaeus, working in his Leyden laboratory, attached an iron rod to a friction machine, then inserted the rod into a jar of water. Still holding the jar, he tried to remove the rod and received a severe shock. The Leyden jar, a storage device for electricity, was born. From there, it

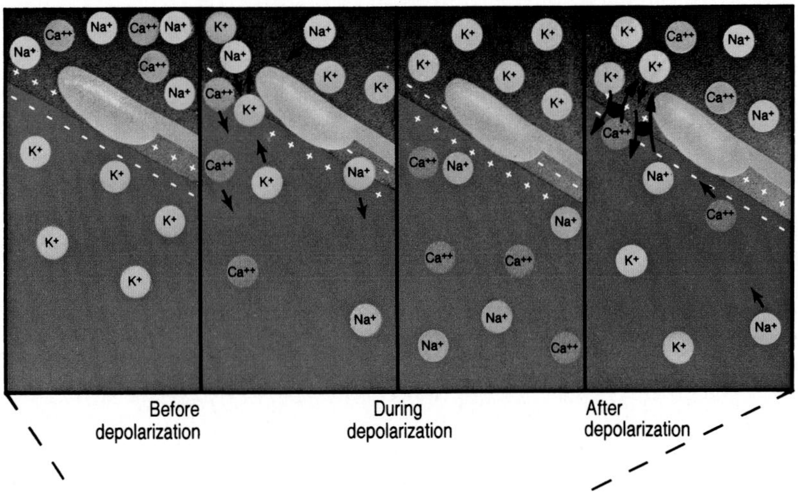

Before
depolarization

During
depolarization

After
depolarization

Contraction's spark jumps from the chemical ebb and flow in the heart's muscle cells. There, the membrane pumps ions — charged atoms — of sodium (Na^+), calcium (Ca^{++}) and potassium (K^+) into and out of the cell. An excess positive charge builds outside the cell, reaching a threshold point. Gates in the membrane fly open, and the ionic flow reverses, spawning an electric current that races from the SA node throughout the heart. This is depolarization, the cellular event that signals contraction in heart muscle. It yields to diastole and repolarization.

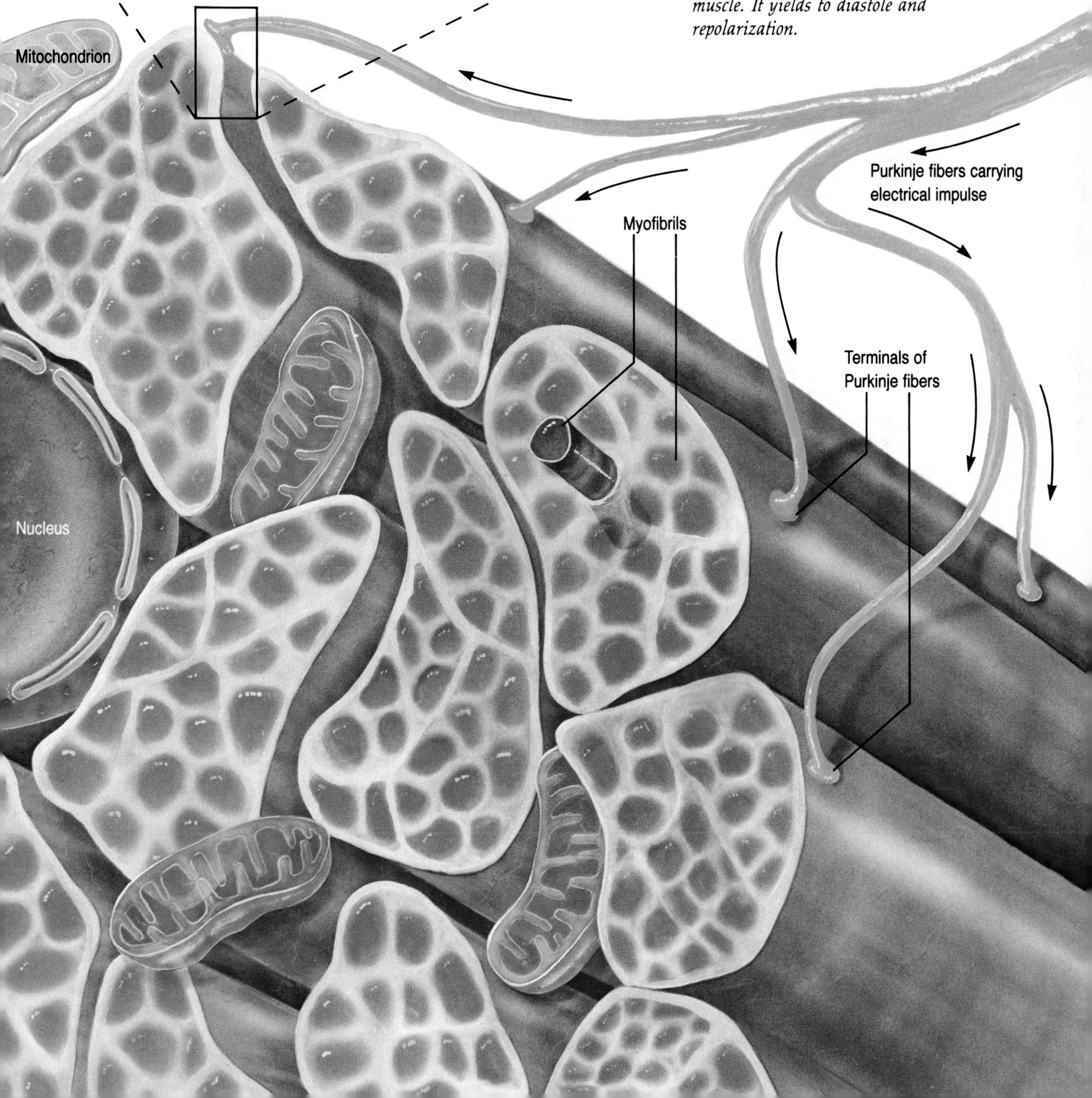

Mitochondrion

Myofibrils

Purkinje fibers carrying
electrical impulse

Terminals of
Purkinje fibers

Nucleus

"I dipped my right hand and left foot into a couple of basins . . . which were connected with the two poles of the electrometer and at once had the pleasure of seeing the mercury column pulsate." So recalled British physiologist, Augustus Waller, of his 1887 electrocardiogram, the first such charting of the heart's labor. Sixteen years later, Dutch physician Willem Einthoven, elaborating on Waller's breakthrough, devised his string galvanometer, left, the prototype of the modern-day electrocardiograph. The technical advances of Waller and Einthoven trace back to experiments carried out in the laboratory of Italian anatomist, Luigi Galvani, opposite. There, about 1790, Galvani, working with frog muscle and electrostatic generators, first proved the existence of "animal electricity."

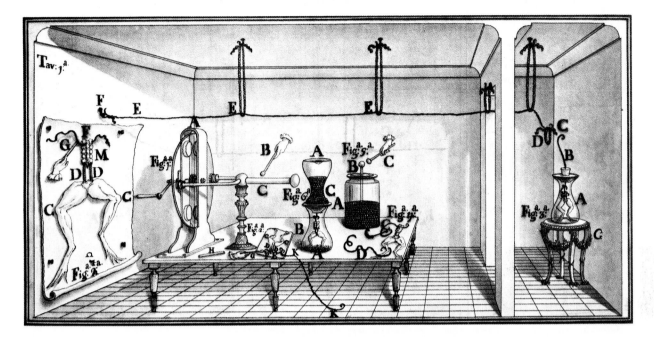

took the curiosity of a Benjamin Franklin to demonstrate the similarity between machine-generated electricity and nature's version. The inventive American flew a kite into a thunderhead, then attached the string to a Leyden jar. Lightning charged the jar.

The time of Galvani and Cunaeus was the eighteenth century; the place, Europe. This was the Enlightenment, the historic crossing upon which science and faith converged. Knowledge flourished, awareness grew, perception changed. The Industrial Revolution dawned and with it came an array of scientific and mechanical advances. Developments in fields such as mathematics, optics and hydraulics aided the deciphering of a formerly mysterious natural world. The closer man looked the more he saw a mechanical basis for life. What made, moved and influenced man, eighteenth-century philosophers believed, were external forces. This revolutionary view of the world became known as mechanism.

A pillar in this rising temple of thought was the concept of immanence, which held that electricity infused all life. Newton, who perceived electricity as an "ether," saw an analogy between a rubbed glass giving off sparks and "ferment in the heart." Writing in 1759, John Wesley,

founder of the Methodist church, viewed electricity as nature's sole spark:

> For in truth there is but one kind of fire in nature, which exists in all places and in all bodies. And this is subtle and active enough . . . to produce and sustain life throughout all nature, as well in animals as in vegetables.

So the spark that first leapt in Galvani's laboratory found ready intellectual tinder. Fellow Italian Alessandro Volta connected stacks of silver, copper, tin and zinc to build the first battery. Soon thereafter, Frenchman André Marie Ampère designed the first instrument to measure electric current. German Johann Schweigger carried Ampère's work a step further and built the first galvanometer. He passed electric current through wires wound on a frame inside of which a magnetic needle spun on a vertical pivot. Italian Leopoldo Nobili refined the galvanometer in 1825, making it sensitive enough to pick up the faint current in a nerve-muscle preparation from a frog. Nobili's countryman, Carlo Matteucci, later attached the instrument to an animal's heart and showed that it generated electricity.

In 1887, British physiologist Augustus Waller recorded the human heart's electrical tracings

*Elastic, energetic heart muscle
thrives on use. Increased blood flow
triggers stronger muscle contraction.
In this way the heart builds stroke
volume — the amount of blood
pumped with each beat.*

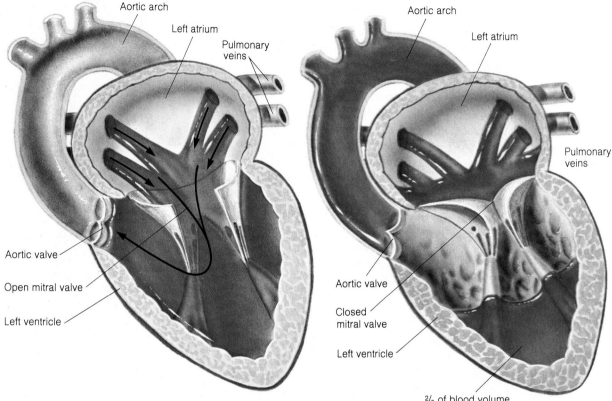

Aortic arch

Left atrium

Pulmonary veins

Aortic valve

Open mitral valve

Left ventricle

Aortic arch

Left atrium

Pulmonary veins

Aortic valve

Closed mitral valve

Left ventricle

²/₅ of blood volume stays in ventricle

without exposing the organ. He strapped electrodes to the back and chest of a subject. A column of mercury rising and falling under the heart's pressure intersected rhythmically with a light beam and created images on photographic plates inching past on the cars of a toy train.

This unorthodox procedure served as inspiration for Dutch physiologist Willem Einthoven. Seeing that electrical activity in the heart was measurable, he also discerned weaknesses in Waller's process. Mercury was an unreliable, inexact gauge, Einthoven believed. Heavy and relatively inert, it overcompensated at the trough and crest of each wave that traced cardiac current. Waller's method rendered only rough readings. In effect it measured electrical potential, not true electrical current.

Einthoven reached back — to Schweigger's galvanometer. He refined it by stringing through a strong magnetic field the finest, lightest conductor he could find: silver-coated quartz filaments only a few millionths of an inch in diameter. Using high magnification, Einthoven photographed a heartbeat's trip across the quartz filament and the resulting wave deflections. The medium's response was quick and exact. Though Einthoven's galvanometer seems elephantine by today's standards — it filled two rooms and took five people to operate — it proved a stunning advance. The string galvanometer, some 100,000 times more sensitive than earlier models, won Einthoven the Nobel Prize in 1924.

Directly descended from Einthoven's two-room, 600-pound brainstorm is a device that today can measure no larger than a briefcase. This is an electrocardiograph, an invaluable diagnostic tool for doctors. Recording the sequence, length and strength of heart muscle action, it yields a detailed image — frame by frame — of the organ's electrical performance. This image is called an electrocardiogram (EKG). The EKG image appears as an irregular line of ink traced by a current-sensing stylus across graph paper. The line usually shows three waves, sequentially known as P, QRS and T. Each stands as a milepost along the heart's contractile route. Respectively, the three waves denote the beginnings of atrial contraction, ventricular contraction and ventricular repolarization. The shape and frequency of the waves tell doctors much about how well the heart is working.

Cardiac Hill and Valley

The trace of the EKG needle, its endless traverse across cardiac hill and valley, measures the beat of the resting, faithful heart. But along this route peaks can suddenly rise, ravines can plunge. These pronounced pulses in the cardiac rhythm are landmarks of the versatile heart, the organ affected by emotion — joy, fear or rage. Under the stress of emotion or vigorous exercise, the healthy heart can increase the amount of blood it pumps about fivefold. Two factors control cardiac output: the organ's frequency of stroke and the volume of blood it can pump with each stroke. To raise its performance, the heart combines increases in both. The central physical element determining output is heart muscle, for it engineers the heart's vital work. Designed for strenuous use, cardiac muscle contracts more forcefully the more it stretches. When active, the body's muscles need more oxygen and therefore process more blood. Blood volume in the veins rises, while muscles around the veins compress, speeding the return of blood to the heart. There, the surge in volume stretches the heart muscle, which responds with a stronger contraction. This forces more blood into the arteries and raises arterial pressure. Nerves leading from the arteries to control centers in the brain transmit the message, and nerves leading back to the heart signal it to pick up the pace.

A healthy heart can raise stroke volume about two-and-a-half times by increasing diastolic capacity and systolic strength. At a resting rate the left ventricle takes in about two-and-a-half ounces of fresh blood to add to its reservoir of two ounces. It ejects the same two-and-a-half

Implanted electrode sends pain or pleasure, depending on how well a rat controls its heart rate. Such tests show that autonomic nervous response is not always involuntary; cardiac control can be learned.

A tiny frog's heart helped German physiologist Otto Loewi unravel the tie between the autonomic nerves and the heart. In his landmark 1921 experiment, Loewi proved that the nerves do not act directly on the heart, but rather secrete chemicals which either inhibit or accelerate it. These, Loewi later identified as acetylcholine and epinephrine, winning him a Nobel Prize in 1936.

ounces with the next stroke. As heart rate rises the organ can process two times as much blood in each half of the cycle, shrinking, in relative terms, its postsystolic reservoir. The more blood the heart can pump with each stroke, the more room it makes for fresh blood on the next beat. High stroke volume is the sign of a well-muscled heart. Marathon runners, swimmers and other athletes often have low pulse rates because their hearts can process a large amount of blood with each stroke. But cardiac fiber has its limits; the athlete's heart cannot build muscle indefinitely.

Skeletal muscle can incur "oxygen debt." It can temporarily stave off the need for oxygen by drawing on stored energy. Heart muscle cannot do this. It demands fresh oxygen with every beat. Oxygen-carrying capillaries richly etch cardiac tissue, while heart cells have many mitochondria, the cellular "powerhouses" that convert nutrients into energy. But there comes a point when the amount of muscle outstrips the capillaries' ability to supply it with oxygen.

To guard against this result and to impose equilibrium, the heart invokes limits. Stroke volume does not rise and fall alone. It does so in tandem with heart rate. Each acts to check the other. Just as stroke volume can overreach, so, too, can heart rate. A heart fluttering at more than 200 beats a minute cannot draw sufficient breath. Filling and stretching incompletely, the hyperactive heart cannot pump blood.

A wide array of factors tempers heart rate. They range from body temperature — each degree of fever raises heart rate by seven-to-ten beats — to hormones and chemicals. Adrenal glands secrete the hormones norepinephrine and epinephrine. Norepinephrine strengthens the contraction of heart muscle and constricts the walls of blood vessels. Epinephrine relaxes the vessels that supply blood to skeletal muscles, which increases the amount of blood delivered during strenuous activity. Hormones traveling in the blood stream can rouse the heart but cannot quiet it. Nor do they act instantaneously. Adrenalin (epinephrine) takes about a minute to stoke up heart rate.

Filling the heart's biological need for quicker, more precise action, the body's nervous system

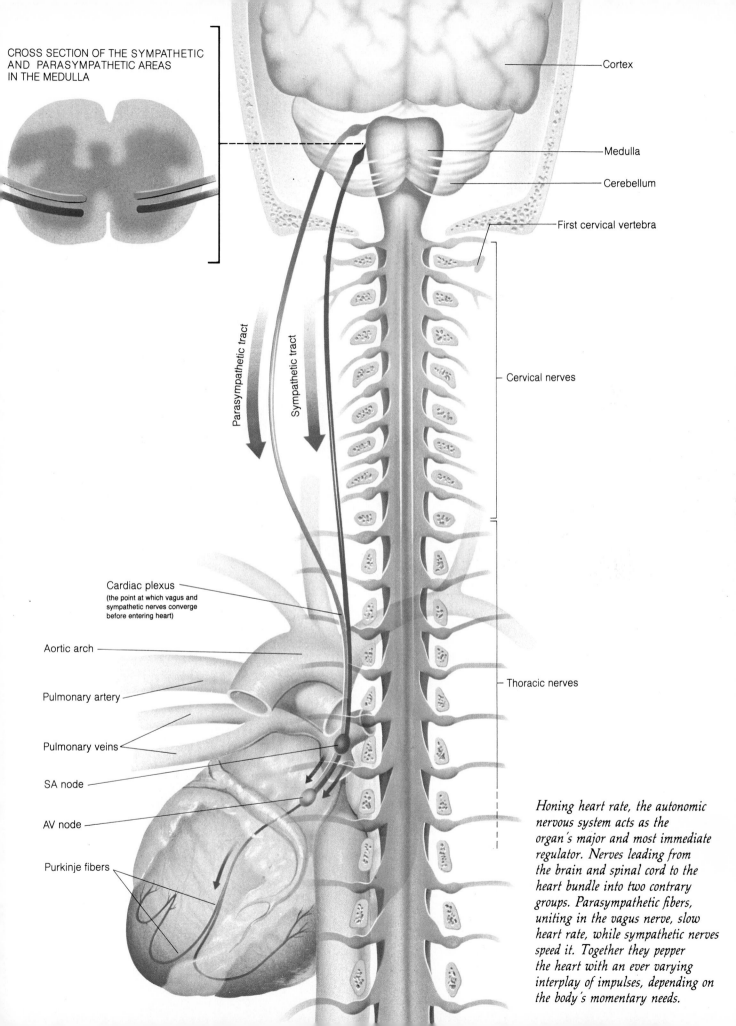

CROSS SECTION OF THE SYMPATHETIC AND PARASYMPATHETIC AREAS IN THE MEDULLA

Cortex

Medulla

Cerebellum

First cervical vertebra

Cervical nerves

Parasympathetic tract

Sympathetic tract

Cardiac plexus
(the point at which vagus and sympathetic nerves converge before entering heart)

Aortic arch

Pulmonary artery

Pulmonary veins

SA node

AV node

Thoracic nerves

Purkinje fibers

Honing heart rate, the autonomic nervous system acts as the organ's major and most immediate regulator. Nerves leading from the brain and spinal cord to the heart bundle into two contrary groups. Parasympathetic fibers, uniting in the vagus nerve, slow heart rate, while sympathetic nerves speed it. Together they pepper the heart with an ever varying interplay of impulses, depending on the body's momentary needs.

Core of the chest, center of life,
the heart connects the cardiovascular
system. Branching into arterioles,
arteries deliver blood to the
nourishing capillaries. Veins
return it — used — to the heart
and lungs. Although three similar
layers form the arterial and venous
walls, below, their consistencies
vary. In arteries, the fibrous tunica
adventitia and muscular tunica
media are thick. Ringing a smooth,
elastic inner layer, they enhance
the passage of blood at high speed
and pressure. Thinner walled veins
readily expand to serve as the body's
low-pressure blood "reservoir."

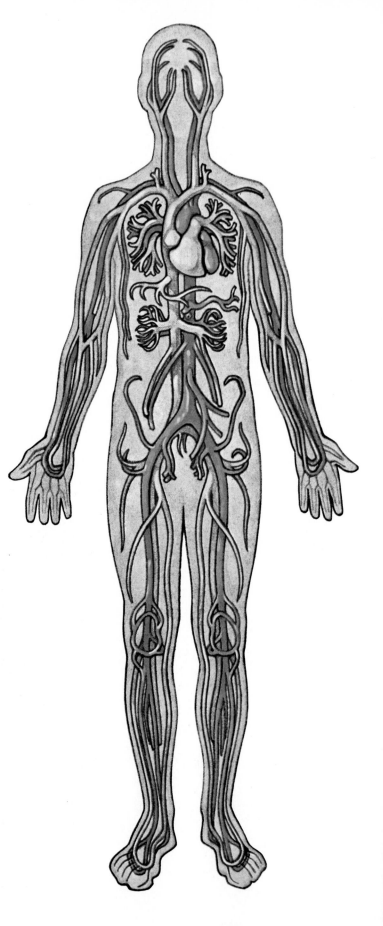

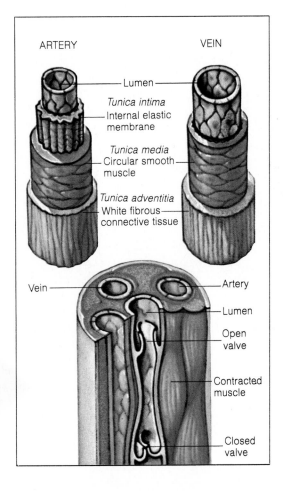

ARTERY   VEIN

Lumen

Tunica intima
Internal elastic
membrane

Tunica media
Circular smooth
muscle

Tunica adventitia
White fibrous
connective tissue

Vein

Artery

Lumen

Open
valve

Contracted
muscle

Closed
valve

acts as the heart's major regulator. Along the length of the spinal cord, nerve fibers sprout and trail outward to touch the internal organs. Together, these neural filaments make up the autonomic nervous system (ANS).

To Quicken and Quell the Heart

The ANS divides into two broad groups of nerves, each a counterbalance to the other. The parasympathetic nervous system acts as the heart's physiological conscience. It slows the heart, counseling it to save energy. Sympathetic nerves do the opposite. They quicken the heart in answer to the challenges that come rushing on the wings of daily experience. Heat, light, love, danger — such stresses force the sympathetic nerves to step in and spend some of the energy the parasympathetics have been husbanding. Both systems reach to the biological core. One conserves the energy necessary for life. The other burns energy when survival demands.

Parasympathetic fibers, uniting as one in the vagus nerve, and sympathetic accelerator nerves from the spine lead to the SA and AV nodes. Sympathetic nerves also spread out and connect with the broader field of heart muscle. Endlessly, each competes for the heart's loyalty. A steady stream of impulses over the vagus nerve holds the heart in check. This is called vagal tone. Cutting vagi nerves in laboratory animals has lifted heart rate to sympathetic heights.

Regulating the autonomic nerves are cells clustered in the heart and along its major arteries. Called baroreceptors, they respond to the rise and fall in blood pressure. Increased pressure, signaling faster heartbeat, stretches these cells, which then flash an impulse to a cardioinhibitor center in the brain. It relays the message along the vagus nerve to the heart. Heart rate slows, and the baroreceptors contract. The vagus nerve then slows its rate of fire. If blood pressure falls sufficiently, sympathetic nerves will flash signals to speed up the heart.

Holding the heart in a finely balanced state, the parasympathetic and sympathetic nerves cast their electrochemical spells. Respectively, they secrete acetylcholine and norepinephrine. The first slows heart rate; the second quickens it.

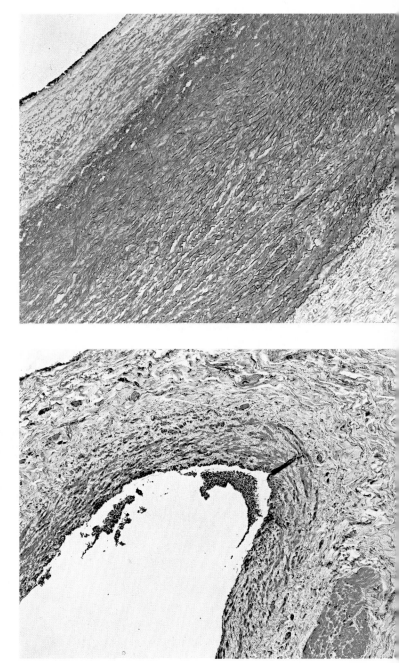

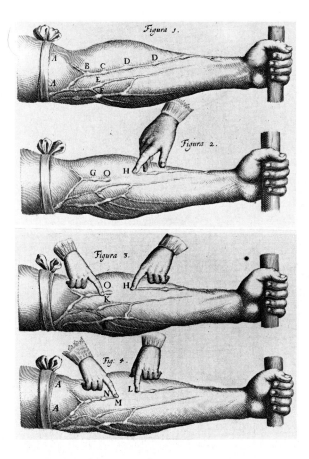

Tourniquet applied, the vessels bulge in this 1628 series of woodcuts illustrating William Harvey's theory that the blood moved in one direction in the veins (Figure 1). With blood pushed back toward the hand, the vein collapses and does not refill (Figure 2). One-way valves (points O and H in Figure 3) were the reason, said Harvey. Proving the point, the released vein refills backward from the lead valve and forward from the rear valve, suggesting that, in the vein, the two valves form a closed chamber holding a given volume of blood (Figure 4).

Each chemical, scientists believe, alters the quality of the membrane in heart cells. The vagal chemical, acetylcholine, allows potassium to flow more easily through the membrane, thereby lengthening the resting potential. Sympathetic fibers increase the flow of sodium across the membrane, inviting a more rapid build-up toward the threshold of depolarization.

The Cardiovascular Chain

High in the chest, deep at the body's core, the heart seems to lie at the quick of life. It hangs like the sun in the sky, and like the sun it suggests a certain detached power. But the fate of the heart is tied to that of other organs, other systems, describing in the end a wide, circling chain of which the heart forges a central link. The chain is the cardiovascular system, 60,000 miles of blood vessels. Wide or narrow, supple yet strong — blood vessels multiply and reach to the deepest crevice of living tissue.

Together the vessels not only oxygenate the tissues and unburden them of wastes, they also serve as stringent regulators of the body's environment. Operating as a thermostat, the vascular system controls the body's temperature, conserving heat or drawing it to the evaporative surface of the skin. It also parcels out blood to the body's disparate tissues and organs — wielding considerable discretion as it does. The heart normally pumps about 15 percent of its output to the skeletal muscles, which constitute about 35 percent of body mass. Under extreme exertion, though, the vessels can move blood from other sources and raise the rate of flow to the muscles by as much as twentyfold.

But the cardiovascular system does more than react to demands of the moment. It also serves a long-term regulatory function. In response to lengthy periods of high oxygen demand by any organ, vessels increase in number and size, channeling blood to where it is needed most. Conversely, low oxygen demand and chronic high blood pressure shrink the vessels in number and diameter. The vascular system appears to reward vitality and penalize inactivity.

The vascular system begins at the aorta, the body's major artery, which arches upward from

William Harvey

Of Motion and Meaning

William Harvey cradled an eel's beating heart in his hands. The heart rocked gently with the force of each contraction, propelling not only blood, but also a stream of thought.

Harvey's first view of a rapidly beating mammal's heart had astonished him. "I all but thought," the seventeenth-century physician later wrote, "that the heart's movement had been understood by God alone." To see the heart's motion clearly, he turned to the study of cold-blooded creatures whose hearts beat more slowly.

Harvey soon realized that the heart played a far different role than that assigned to it by Galen 1,500 years earlier. In Galen's view, the heart acted as a furnace, sucking blood into its chambers and heating it to warm the body. The liver replenished the blood burned up in the heart. Harvey detected a subtle difference in the heart's movement. It did not expand to draw blood in; it contracted to push blood out. The heart was a pump.

Once Harvey identified the heart's true motion, he quickly made other discoveries. His teacher, Fabricius, had noticed "little doors" in the veins but had never learned their function. Harvey suspected that the valves governed the

direction of blood flow. A simple but ingenious experiment bolstered his theory. He tried to push a probe through a vein from the direction of the heart and found its passage was quickly obstructed. When pushed toward the heart, the probe moved easily. The valves opened for it.

Harvey then tied a knot around a snake's main artery. Blood backed up in the heart, eventually rupturing it. He repeated the experiment, this time cutting the artery between the knot and the heart. Blood spurted out in time with the heartbeat.

Harvey used a similar method to study the movement of blood in man. He wrapped a tourniquet tightly around the arm. The veins below the restricting bandage, unable to move blood to the heart, bulged in bold relief. Harvey

pressed a vein, emptying it of blood. The blood reentered the vein only from the end most distant from the heart. Blood, he concluded, did not flow back and forth in the vessels like a tide. Arteries channeled the rushing stream of blood away from the heart; veins carried it back.

Having revealed the blood's one-way path, Harvey used a set of simple calculations to support his findings. He estimated that every beat of the heart pumped two ounces of blood. The average human heart beat seventy-two times a minute, so in one hour the heart pumped 8,640 ounces — about 540 pounds — of blood. The liver could not produce this quantity of blood in an hour, Harvey realized, nor could the body contain it. The same blood was used over and over again — it circulated.

In 1628, after twelve years of experiments with over eighty species of animals, Harvey published *Exercitatio anatomica de motu cordis,* An Anatomical Essay on the Motion of the Heart. He prefaced his monumental contribution to medicine with a comparatively modest statement of intent: "to contribute something pleasing to good men and appropriate to learned ones, and of service to literature."

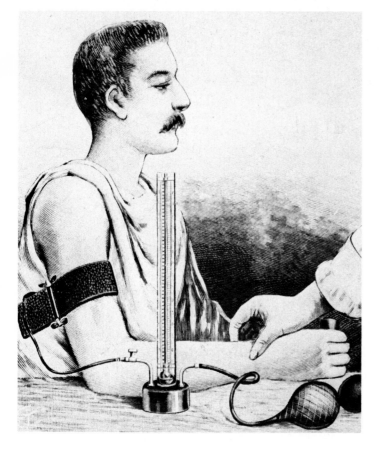

Prototype of the current blood pressure gauge, the sphygmomanometer, above, yielded a finer reading than its predecessors. Developed by Italian physician Riva-Rocci in 1896, it used a mercury column as a gauge.

the left ventricle. It branches and rebranches like an ancient oak, arteries dividing into small arteries, then into arterioles that ultimately flourish into billions of capillaries. This is the arterial system, purveyor of fresh blood, messenger of life. The venous system, hinged at the capillaries to the arteries, forms the return half of this closed loop. Retrieving blood spent of its oxygen, tiny venules merge into small veins, which, in turn, collect into larger veins. These finally unite in the venae cavae, the body's two major veins, which spill used blood into the right atrium.

Balance and Tension

The nourishing arteries and relieving veins are like systole and diastole, like heart rate and volume. Inextricable elements of balance, together they assure life. The fine balance of the system extends to form as well as function. Artery walls have three layers which, moving from inside out, graduate from elastic to rigid. Large arteries absorb surges of blood coursing from the heart, expand with the swelling force, then snap back to urge the fluid on its way. As the blood moves down the arterial tree, the need for speed surpasses the need for force. Gradually the consistency of the artery walls evolves from fibrous to smooth, easing the vital flow of blood. Arterioles, the last leg in this delivery system, act as control valves through which blood moves into the capillaries. The well-muscled arteriole wall gives the vessel flexibility. To flood capillaries feeding oxygen-starved tissue, an arteriole can dilate to increase blood flow by as much as 400 percent.

The veins, returning blood to the heart, constitute a cardiovascular reservoir. They outnumber arteries and accordingly hold a larger share of the circulating blood, about 65 percent. They stand ready to supply the heart. Less muscular but more elastic than arteries, veins also have thinner walls and lower internal pressure. To compensate for this lack of dynamic force, they lie sheathed in skeletal muscle. The slightest shift of a limb squeezes the vein and drives the blood toward the heart. To fix blood on its course, veins have many semilunar valves, particularly in the legs and arms. These swing open ahead of each pulse of blood, then snap shut to prevent back flow.

The cardiovascular system thrives in a state of high tension, a condition created by two opposing forces. One is blood pressure, the force the fluid exerts on the vessel wall. The second is peripheral resistance, the grasp of muscle around vein or artery. When the muscle constricts, it squeezes the vessel. Blood pressure is measured by the height to which the blood's internal force can raise a column of mercury. Highest in the aorta, where it averages around 100 millimeters and can leap as high as 200, blood pressure drops as the blood progresses on its journey away from the heart. Blood is said to flow down a "blood pressure hill." Pressure drops to around 35 millimeters by the time the arterioles branch into capillaries and falls another 20 millimeters by the time the capillaries connect to the venules. In the venae cavae, the final leg of the cardiovascular cycle, blood pressure registers near zero.

Zero blood pressure in a large vein is not abnormal, but the same reading in an artery could prove fatal to the tissue it feeds. Veins can expand to about eight times the size of arteries and hold three times as much blood. Conversely, in arterioles, where blood flow is slight, pressure dropping below 20 millimeters cannot match the force of the muscle in the vessel wall. The vessel

Having thrust a glass tube into a horse's artery, Stephen Hales performs an early blood pressure experiment in 1731. The fluid's rise in the column reflects the force it exerts on the artery wall. "Insensibly led on" to study both plant and animal hydraulics, Hales conducted many crude yet fruitful experiments. Minister as well as physiologist, he reveled in such scientific tinkering "since the wonderful works of the Author of nature are so fruitful in furnishing us . . . with fresh matter for our researches."

Stephen Hales

A Measure of Force

The discovery of circulation traced the blood's surging force to the pumping action of the heart. But little was known about the force itself until Stephen Hales, an eighteenth-century English pastor, made the first accurate measurements of blood pressure.

Hales developed his passion for science while attending Cambridge University. There he became very friendly with William Stukeley, another student and an enthusiastic amateur scientist. Single-minded in his pursuit of anatomical knowledge, young Stukeley had relieved his cat "of the infirmities of age" to get the skeleton. Hales and Stukeley chased butterflies, identified plants and dissected local wildlife. After graduating, Hales became pastor of St. Mary's Church in Teddington, a village on the Thames. The parish demanded little of his time, leaving Hales free to pursue his scientific studies.

"In December I caused a Mare to be tied down alive on her Back," wrote Hales in an account of an early blood pressure experiment. He exposed an artery in the mare's upper leg and tied it off. He then fit a brass pipe into the artery, attaching it to a glass tube which towered nine feet above the horse's body. His appara-

tus in place, Hales untied the knot restricting the artery. Blood rushed into the glass tube, rising with each pulse by as much as a foot. It finally reached a height of eight feet, three inches and continued to pulsate with each heartbeat.

Hales drained a quart of blood from the artery, then replaced the glass tube to test the pressure. The more blood he drained, the more the pressure dropped. After seventeen quarts had been removed, the pressure in the tube was so low that the blood rose only two feet. The mare broke out in a cold sweat and died.

Deeply disturbed by his work with live animals, Hales turned to the similar but less gruesome study of the pressure of sap in plants. In 1727, he published *Vegetable Staticks,* which became the forerunner of modern plant physiology.

Its success led him to resume his animal experiments. In 1733, Hales compiled his findings in a volume entitled, in part, *Haemastaticks,* an account of some "Hydraulick and Hydrostatical" experiments on the blood vessels of animals.

The book describes eleven experiments, comparing the blood pressures of several animal species. Hales found that the hearts of small animals worked harder, pumping proportionately more blood than the hearts of larger animals. But larger animals, he learned, had higher blood pressure. Their blood traveled a greater distance and, therefore, met greater resistance in the blood vessels. Using calculations derived from these experiments, Hales estimated that the blood pressure of man would support a column of blood seven-and-one-half feet high. His estimate was high but remarkably accurate, considering the crude method he used.

He deftly moved between the worlds of dutiful minister and daring scientist. The transition was easy; he saw one job as an extension of the other. The study of the works of God, Hales told his readers, revealed "the Signatures of his Wisdom and Power . . . because in every Thing we see a wise Design."

collapses to a point where red blood cells can no longer squeeze through the narrowed opening.

The heart is a generous organ. It showers the system it powers with an excess of energy — too much blood. The aorta takes the overflow and bulges wildly, its blood pressure zooming as the left ventricle contracts. The aorta's walls then spring back to push blood through the arteries. In this way the aorta and its major branches act as subsidiary pumps to the heart. Forcing these pumps into action is a group of arterioles in the abdomen. The arteries up above must work hard to push blood through the small arterioles.

Blood rushes out of the heart, traveling about a foot a second, and courses down the arterial tree, losing velocity as it goes. By the time it reaches the arterioles, near the end of the arterial line, blood has slowed to less than an inch a second. In the capillaries it travels at about a fiftieth of an inch per second.

A given volume of blood takes about twenty seconds to travel the entire cardiovascular circuit. It spends about a second, 5 percent of the time, in the capillaries. But these tiny tubes are only a millimeter or so long. Thus, relative to their length, relative to the pace at which the blood travels through them, they hold the blood for a comparatively long time. Capillaries are built to supply and nourish; arteries, to deliver. Densely walled, high-pressure, high-speed tubes, arteries rush the blood to the capillaries. There the blood trades vital oxygen for carbon dioxide, urea and other chemical wastes.

To maximize the exchange, capillary walls are gossamer-thin and highly permeable. Some of these vessels are so narrow they force blood cells to inch through one at a time. Capillaries constitute an army whose strength lies in numbers. As the distance along the arterial tree grows, the cross-sectional area of the arteries increases. The total diameter of the arterioles exceeds that of the arteries. Dwarfing both is the combined surface area of the capillaries, which totals about 60,000 square feet, larger than a football field.

Veins taking blood home to the heart connect with the arteries that brought it out. The two halves of the cardiovascular system close this vital circle and so define the heart's perfect unity.

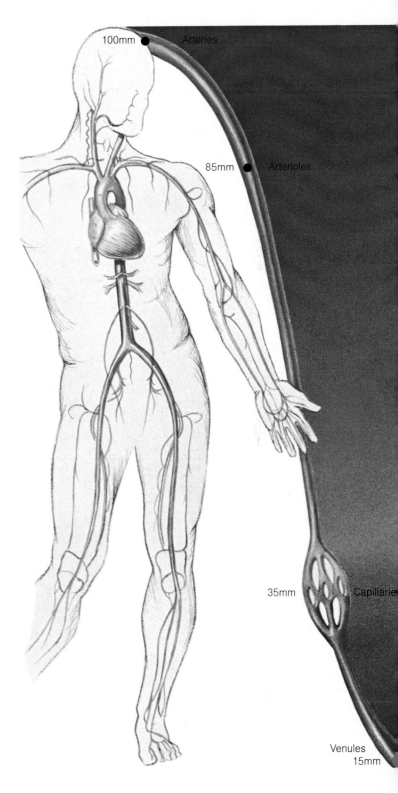

100mm — Arteries

85mm — Arterioles

35mm — Capillaries

Venules 15mm

Chapter 4

The Coronary Puzzle

It can strike with the savage, paralyzing force of a sledgehammer. Or it may pass so quietly its victim remains oblivious to the damage it has wreaked. Days, weeks, even years in advance, it might warn of its approach. But all too often it arrives unannounced and unexpected. Although it preys on the middle-aged male with a singular fury, no gender, race, age group or economic class is left untouched.

Four thousand times a day, one-and-a-half million times a year, in homes, offices and automobiles, on street corners and subways, the grim drama of a heart attack is replayed. Seemingly sudden, a heart attack is actually the final stage in a process that has been years in the making. Nearly all heart attacks result from an insidious disorder known as coronary heart disease.

Epidemic since the early 1900s, coronary heart disease claims half a million American lives each year. Two-and-a-half million people are disabled by it. The annual economic cost — a measure of medical expenses, salaries and workdays lost — runs into tens of billions of dollars.

For more than thirty years, scientists have been trying to piece together the coronary puzzle. The leading clues have come from worldwide population studies. From such investigations has emerged a pattern portraying coronary heart disease as a modern affliction, a disease of affluence. Although it kills a large percentage of the world's population, coronary heart disease plunders only prosperous nations. In most undeveloped countries, the disease rarely occurs. But recent statistics indicate that some of the puzzle has been pieced together. While heart disease is still the leading cause of death in the United States, the death rate from heart attacks has declined. After a sharp upward trend beginning in 1920 and peaking in the mid-1960s, heart attack deaths have declined by more than 30 percent. Sixty percent of the decline has taken place since 1973.

Like a puzzle's discordant piece, the rounded heart lies amidst hard-edged forms in Paul Klee's painting, Ab Ovo. Scientists today tirelessly sift and assemble an array of clues in the search to solve the modern riddle — and epidemic — of coronary heart disease.

A blaze of polarized light lays bare the translucent beauty of a cholesterol crystal, here magnified 400 times. Although it is essential to life, too much cholesterol can endanger the heart.

Coronary heart disease results from the narrowing of arteries that nourish the heart. When coronary arteries are healthy, their linings smooth and clear, they carry a steady stream of blood. Too often, however, their inner walls become rough and thick, like rust in a water pipe. Deposits of cholesterol, connective tissue and smooth muscle cells build up, beginning the deadly process known as atherosclerosis — hardening of the arteries. These deposits, called atherosclerotic plaques, can eventually clog an artery completely. Some doctors believe that an arterial wall must be wounded by injury or disease before plaques can form. But whatever the cause, when clogged coronary arteries cut off the blood supply to the heart, heart muscle dies and a heart attack is the inevitable result.

Doctors are still not sure what causes plaques to form. But through studies of family medical histories, diet and social habits, they have been able to identify certain factors that appear to increase a person's chances of developing coronary heart disease. Some risk factors — gender, age, predisposing illnesses like diabetes, a strong family history of heart disease — cannot be altered. Others can be reduced or eliminated. Elevated levels of cholesterol and other blood fats, smoking, high blood pressure, obesity, stress, lack of exercise, consumption of excess sugar and alcohol and certain personality traits can be altered.

Much of the research identifying risk factors stems from a single study. In 1948, a group of public health officials from the National Heart Institute arrived in Framingham, Massachusetts, a suburb of Boston chosen for its broad mix of ethnic, social and economic groups. Still in existence, the Framingham project is the largest long-term study of heart disease ever conducted.

The research team selected a large sample of residents with no sign of coronary heart disease. From Framingham's 1948 population of 28,000, the researchers chose as participants 2,282 men and 2,845 women between the ages of thirty and sixty-two. Each subject underwent blood tests, X-rays, electrocardiograph readings and blood pressure examinations. Those who met the stringent requirements were asked to supply a record of their living habits and medical history.

Framingham doctors examined the participants every two years for signs of heart trouble and interviewed their family physicians regularly. When a member of the study died, researchers sought permission for an autopsy to determine the condition of the heart and coronary arteries. Over the years, a stream of cautiously worded reports has flowed from the project's headquarters. The basic message to Americans concerned about heart disease is smoke less, exercise regularly, maintain normal weight, reduce dietary fats and get treatment for high blood pressure.

The Cholesterol Connection

Many experts believe that the willingness of Americans to heed such advice has contributed significantly to the recent drop in heart attack deaths. Absolute proof linking all of these factors with atherosclerosis has not been established, however, and the effects of some have been disputed. At the center of one of the most heated controversies is cholesterol.

A soapy, waxy chemical found in all body tissues, cholesterol is one of four types of lipids, fatty substances in the blood stream. It is essential in the production of nerve tissue, bile and certain hormones. In addition to extracting the chemical from foods, the body manufactures its own cholesterol in the liver. The more cholesterol a person consumes, the less the body produces. Reduced consumption spurs the body to increase production. This feedback process helps regulate blood cholesterol levels. If a person's diet contains large amounts of cholesterol, the excess may find its way into the lining of the arteries and contribute to the formation of plaques.

Serum cholesterol, the amount of cholesterol present in the blood stream, is measured in terms of milligrams per deciliter of blood, expressed as mg/dl. Atherosclerosis rarely occurs when the serum cholesterol level is below 200 mg/dl and is very common when levels are above 300 mg/dl.

Because it is insoluble in blood, cholesterol circulates through the blood stream bound to lipoproteins, molecules containing both protein and fat. Like microscopic cargo vessels, lipoproteins sail through the blood stream with their load of cholesterol. Recent findings suggest that there

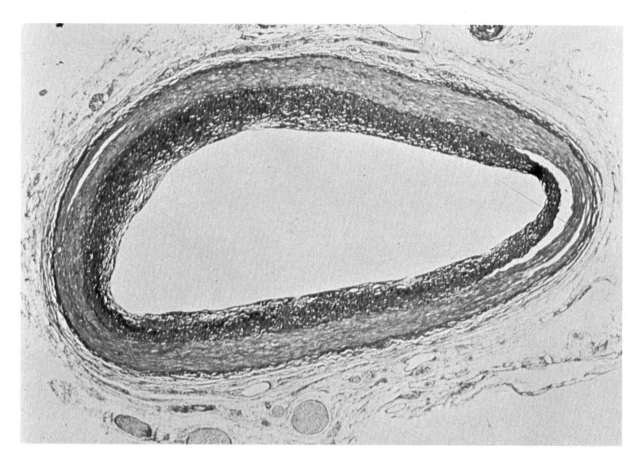

may be both good and bad lipoproteins. Low-density lipoproteins (LDLs) are richest in cholesterol. High LDL levels have been closely linked with atherosclerosis. The good members of the lipoprotein family are the small, heavy, high-density lipoproteins (HDLs). Some scientists think that HDLs clear away fat from artery walls and return it to the liver for excretion.

German pathologist Rudolph Virchow made the first connection between atherosclerosis and diet more than a hundred years ago. Laboratory experiments with rabbits confirmed his theory that high levels of cholesterol in food could cause plaques to form on the walls of coronary arteries. Additional research in the nineteenth century revealed that concentrations of blood fats could be altered by changes in diet. In more recent studies, rhesus monkeys, who normally consume minimal amounts of cholesterol and saturated fats, were switched to a high-cholesterol, high-fat diet. Plaques formed in their coronary arteries. When the animals resumed their normal diet, the lesions began to heal.

While human studies have not shown such a clear cause-and-effect relationship, a striking statistical correlation between dietary cholesterol and heart disease has been established. During World War II, Northern Europe suffered a shortage of meat and dairy products. At the same time, the region's heart attack death rate declined dramatically. After the war, when foods rich in cholesterol and saturated fats once again became available, the death rate rose to prewar levels.

A major international study conducted in the fifties and sixties revealed a high incidence of coronary heart disease in countries with diets containing large quantities of animal fats. The United States and Finland, both consumers of huge quantities of milk, led all nations. The lowest rate occurred in Japan, where relatively little

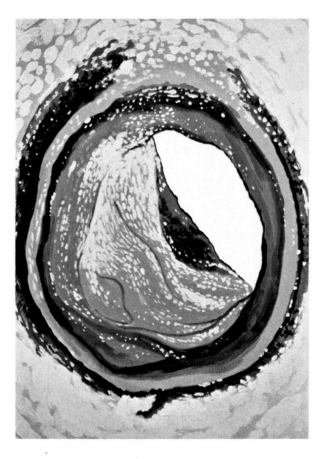

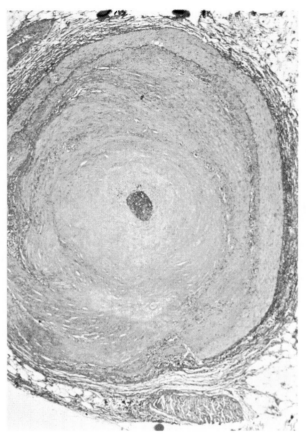

fat is eaten. In Greece, where the people consume many fatty foods, there was a surprisingly low heart disease rate. But only 8 percent of the Greeks' total caloric intake came from animal fats. Most of it was derived from olive oil and other vegetable oils high in polyunsaturated fats. Saturated fats, found mostly in butter and lard, are chemically "filled," meaning they cannot accept any more hydrogen molecules. Polyunsaturated fats, which predominate in most vegetable oils, can add hydrogen atoms at more than one place on their atomic chain.

Through a blood sample, a doctor can tell how efficiently a patient's body uses cholesterol and other fats. An especially valuable test is the measure of lipoprotein levels. Physicians consider the ratio of HDLs to LDLs an important index of heart disease risk. At least a dozen studies have shown that the risk of heart disease increases as HDL levels decrease. Statistics from Framingham

Thin as a soda-straw, the coronary arteries funnel life-sustaining blood to the heart. Cleaving to artery walls, plaques block blood flow and set the stage for a heart attack. Opposite, a cross section of an artery taken from a hundred-year-old woman reveals an absence of plaques. A painted slide, above left, shows a diseased, narrowed artery, its thickened walls creating a bottleneck for heartbound blood. Above right, blood clot forms a deadly bull's eye in this plaque-scarred artery from a fifty-nine-year-old hypertensive woman who suffered a heart attack seven weeks before she died.

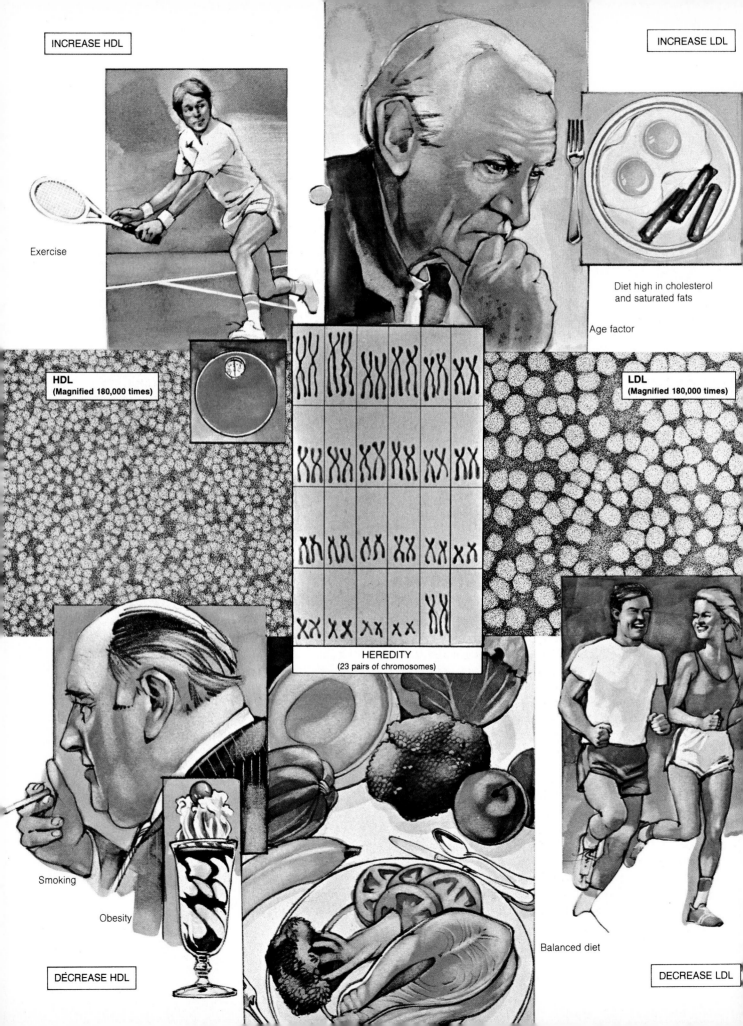

INCREASE HDL

Exercise

INCREASE LDL

Diet high in cholesterol
and saturated fats

Age factor

HDL
(Magnified 180,000 times)

LDL
(Magnified 180,000 times)

HEREDITY
(23 pairs of chromosomes)

Smoking

Obesity

Balanced diet

DECREASE HDL

DECREASE LDL

Exercise, good eating habits and hereditary fortune can elevate the blood serum levels of HDLs, the helpful lipoproteins. A surplus of LDLs, however, may increase the risk of heart attack.

reveal that a fifty-five-year-old man with an HDL level of 65 mg/dl is only half as likely to develop atherosclerosis as a man of the same age, habits and blood pressure whose HDL level is only 45 mg/dl.

Raising HDLs

Can a person raise his HDL level? While scientists have no definitive answers, the evidence leans toward a qualified yes. Low HDL levels have been found in smokers and in people who are obese or sedentary. It would seem possible, then, that changing such habits might boost HDL levels. Both male and female marathon runners appear to have an abundance of HDLs. In one study, runners averaged about 20 mg/dl higher in HDLs than subjects who led physically inactive lives. A recent Texas study comparing 200 marathon runners, joggers and sedentary men found that those who ran the farthest daily had the highest levels of HDLs. Surprisingly, the distance a person ran proved a better predictor of HDL levels than smoking, diet or weight. According to one theory, prolonged exercise somehow increases the activity of an enzyme that helps create more HDLs.

The Framingham team also concluded that moderate drinkers have higher HDLs than those who abstain or drink heavily. Gender is another factor. Until menopause, women show consistently higher concentrations of HDLs than men, which might account for their lower rates of heart disease. Heredity may also play a role. One researcher found very high HDL levels — above 75 mg/dl — in families with a history of longevity. Such families have members who live to age eighty or ninety without developing coronary heart disease.

Finland, which has a diet rich in dairy products, also has one of the world's highest death rates from heart attack. Researchers set out to discover whether a switch to a low-fat diet would improve Finnish cardiovascular health. Study subjects drank a "filled" milk containing soybean oil in skim milk and ate margarine instead of butter. The results were dramatic. The serum cholesterol level of those on the low-fat diet fell about 15 percent. Men on the diet suf-

fered only half as many deaths from coronary heart disease as those in a control group eating typically Finnish fare. Women on the low-fat diet had one-third fewer deaths. When some of the subjects in the low-fat group resumed the fatty diet, the serum cholesterol in their blood returned to previously high levels, and many developed coronary heart disease.

As persuasive as such studies seem, a significant segment of the medical community remains skeptical about the role of cholesterol in heart disease. The test for determining cholesterol levels is subject to perhaps more errors than any other laboratory test. Anxiety can affect the test outcome by as much as 100 percent, resulting in a false high or low reading. It is also difficult to separate the role of diet from other habits and traits which may affect the heart. While many studies show a link between reductions in dietary cholesterol and a drop in heart attacks, other studies have not found a strong correlation. As a result, many physicians have begun to recommend dietary changes only for those patients whose cholesterol levels are abnormally high, or when other risk factors are also present.

The Risks of Sugar

Cholesterol and saturated fats are not the only dietary elements linked with heart disease. Another suspected villain is refined sugar. Many people who consume large quantities of sugar have high blood levels of triglycerides, another fat implicated in the formation of plaques. In one study, British biochemist John Yudkin discovered that people who ate four or more ounces of refined sugar a day suffered heart attacks at a rate five times greater than those eating just two-and-a-half ounces. But in Cuba, Honduras and Costa Rica, where sugar consumption is very high, heart disease rates remain low.

Sugar does cause grave cardiovascular damage in at least one group of people. Diabetes mellitus is a disorder in which the body does not produce enough insulin, a hormone that burns sugar. The resulting unburned sugar creates an excess of plaque-forming triglycerides. The rate of heart attack among diabetics is at least three times greater than among nondiabetics.

Despite controversy over the role of cholesterol in heart disease, most experts caution against an overly rich diet. The still-life paintings, above and right, are a study in gastronomic contrasts. The opulent splendor of Un Dessert, above, by Dutch artist Jan Davidsz de Heem, masks its simple fare of fruits. Except for the fruit pie in the center, de Heem's banquet is free of cholesterol and fat. The meal of duck, meat pie and biscuits in Jean Chardin's Still Life, right, is relatively high in saturated fats and cholesterol.

In the past, doctors put diabetic patients on low-carbohydrate diets. Recently, scientists have found that a diet high in carbohydrates often helps to control the disease and may reduce the risk of atherosclerosis. Now, most diabetics are permitted as much as 60 percent of their total calories in carbohydrates, as long as refined sugars and total daily calories are restricted.

Nutritional guidelines for the diabetic are very similar to those the American Heart Association recommends for anyone trying to reduce the risk of coronary heart disease. The basic goals are to limit sugar, cholesterol and saturated fats. The typical American consumes from 400 to 800 milligrams of cholesterol a day. This amount can be reduced to less than 300 milligrams — which the AHA considers a safe upper limit — by cutting down on fatty meats, whole milk dairy products, cooking oils made from saturated fats and cholesterol-rich egg yolks. Levels of triglycerides can be kept to a safe minimum by limiting the "simple" sugars found in sweets and snack foods. In general, the coronary-conscious diet contains fewer fat meats, dairy foods and sweets, and more poultry, seafood, vegetables, fruits and whole grains. In a healthy diet, roughly 15 percent of calories should come from protein, 50 percent from carbohydrates and 35 percent from fat. The recommended ratio of polyunsaturates to saturated fats is roughly two to one.

Some researchers, however, have found evidence that polyunsaturates may be dangerous, especially when consumption exceeds 10 percent of total calories. Studies have linked them with blood disease, cancer, liver damage and vitamin deficiencies. In an eight-year experiment conducted at a Los Angeles veterans' hospital, a group of patients whose diet contained four times as many polyunsaturates as a second group had 60 percent more cancers.

That diet may not be the sole or most important factor in maintaining a healthy heart surfaced in a classic study begun in 1963. Researchers at the Harvard School of Public Health joined with scientists at Trinity College in Dublin, Ireland. They hoped to find reasons why Irish immigrants living in the United States for ten years or more experienced heart disease at the

same rate as native-born Americans. At the time of the study, the heart attack rate in the United States was four times greater than in Ireland.

The immigrants chosen for the study all had brothers living in Ireland. This factor enabled the scientists to rule out hereditary differences. Comparing electrocardiograms, blood pressure readings and cholesterol levels, the researchers discovered that the cardiovascular condition of the brothers in Ireland was far superior to that of the American immigrants. Autopsies performed on subjects who died during the course of the study revealed that the hearts and arteries of the American brothers had aged from fifteen to twenty-eight years more rapidly.

Most astonishing of all, the Irish participants consumed a diet much richer in fats and cholesterol than that of the Americans. If cholesterol were the major factor affecting coronary health, the Irish brothers would have been less healthy.

What was the explanation? "The Irishmen have muscles and they're using them," answered Harvard's Frederick Stare, a member of the research team. The Irishmen worked longer and harder, walked more and used their muscles to perform chores their American brothers would not attempt without power tools. "It seems evi-

dent," concluded Stare, "that physical activity prevents the build-up of cholesterol by burning saturated fats."

Scientific studies have produced conflicting evidence about the role of exercise in preventing heart attacks or prolonging life, but there is no doubt that physical fitness benefits the cardiovascular system. Exercise can also help reduce other risk factors. Levels of protective HDLs probably rise with vigorous exercise while harmful fats like triglycerides and LDLs are burned up during physical activity. Exercise also reduces excess body weight, an indirect risk factor. A leaner body reduces demands on the heart. Active people often have lower blood pressure as well. In fact, exercise alone can sometimes control high blood pressure.

Cardiovascular Conditioning

The best conditioning for the cardiovascular system is aerobic, or dynamic, exercise. Swimming, bicycling, cross-country skiing, running and jumping rope are aerobic. All of these activities involve large groups of muscles engaged in repetitive activity. Working muscles require more energy than resting muscles. Oxygen, needed to transform nutrients into energy, is pumped to the muscles by the heart. To meet increased demands for oxygen, the heart must pump more blood. When an average adult is at rest, the heart may pump four or five quarts each minute at a pulse rate of 60 to 100. Intense exertion can send the pulse rate soaring to 200 or more.

The heart of an inactive person has a small pumping capacity, limiting his ability to exercise for prolonged periods. With training, the heart muscle grows stronger. Each heartbeat, or contraction, becomes more vigorous, pumping a greater volume of blood to the body. The heart of a distance runner can elevate its pumping capacity to five or six times its output at rest. The runner's resting heart rate is superior, too — perhaps two-thirds that of a sedentary person — which means less work for his heart. A stronger heart also pumps more efficiently, helping to deliver more blood to working muscles whose demand is high, and less to inactive areas of the body. One of the best indicators of cardiovascular fitness is the amount of oxygen the lungs can deliver to muscles and other body cells at peak activity. This level, measured on a treadmill test, increases steadily with regular exercise as the heart grows stronger. Exercise improves the elasticity of the arteries and might stimulate the growth of added blood vessels to the heart. These collateral vessels provide another route for blood should the coronary arteries become clogged.

Strenuous exercise does not always ensure a healthy heart. It can sometimes lead to sudden death. When Stanford University researchers studied the medical histories of eighteen people who had died during or just after jogging, they found evidence of coronary heart disease in thirteen cases. Three of the remaining five had died from other heart-related causes.

Aside from undiagnosed coronary heart disease, certain heart irregularities can spell danger for the exercise enthusiast. Ventricular fibrillation, irregular contractions of the ventricles, can cause sudden death. While people with known coronary problems have a great risk of suffering fibrillation, the healthy sometimes fall victim as well. Another cause of death while exercising is hypertrophy, a thickening of the heart muscles which can hamper the flow of blood through the chambers of the heart. An abnormal, hereditary "bridge" of tissue can also cause sudden death. Passing just above the coronary artery, this tissue can suddenly constrict the artery during a heart contraction and cut off blood flow.

An exercise electrocardiogram, also called a stress test, can sometimes identify people whose hearts might respond abnormally, even fatally, to vigorous exercise. Certain heart irregularities which might not show up during a resting EKG may be detected. During a stress test, the patient pedals a stationary bicycle, walks on a treadmill or climbs a staircase while the electrocardiograph traces the heart's reaction. Since atherosclerosis often remains without symptoms for years, most doctors recommend that adults with a high risk of heart disease take a stress test before starting an exercise program. A stress test determines the overall fitness level of the cardiovascular system and is often used to set the pace and limits of an individual's exercise program. One of its major functions is to measure the maximum amount of oxygen the body can utilize. As the patient exhales into a canvas bag, a computer records the amount of oxygen absorbed each minute.

Another important fitness indicator measured by the stress test is the maximum heart rate —

the fastest rate at which the heart can beat and still supply adequate oxygen to working muscles. The goal of any exercise program designed to improve the cardiovascular system is to attain 70 to 85 percent of this maximum rate and sustain it for twenty to thirty minutes. It may take weeks or months to work up to this level, depending on one's physical condition.

The Silent Killer

In the United States and other countries that have seen recent declines in heart attack deaths, authorities give much of the credit to improved treatment and identification of people suffering from hypertension, or high blood pressure. Statistics from the Framingham study indicate that coronary heart disease is three to five times more common among people with hypertension. The arteries leading to the brain are particularly vulnerable to damage from high blood pressure. Stroke afflicts untreated hypertensives four times more frequently than people who have normal blood pressure. Hypertension takes a heavy toll on the kidneys as well, damaging their blood vessels until they can no longer perform their vital waste-clearing function.

About thirty-five million Americans suffer from hypertension. For unknown reasons, high blood pressure affects about twice as many blacks as whites in the United States. Because hypertension frequently has no symptoms until its advanced stages, a sufferer may feel healthy and vigorous for years, yet run an extremely high risk of stroke, heart disease and kidney ailments.

High blood pressure forces the heart to pump harder than normal because the increased velocity of blood flowing through the arteries creates resistance that the heart must overcome. Eventually, this overwork makes the arteries stiff and brittle. To meet the increasing workload, the heart may add muscle fibers, which places an additional burden on the heart. Eventually, the overworked heart may fail. Before the advent of drugs to control hypertension, heart failure was the most frequent cause of death among people suffering from high blood pressure.

To take a patient's blood pressure, the doctor measures the height to which the force of blood

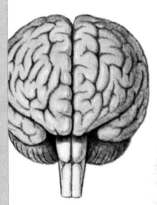

Exercise stimulates centers in the brain that increase heart rate

Blood capillaries in the muscles enlarge

Left heart

Sympathetic nerves and circulating hormones dilate coronary arteries. This increases oxygen supply and acts directly on heart muscles, accelerating its metabolism and increasing force of contraction

Right heart

Sympathetic nerve stimulation and circulating hormones, plus relative decrease in vagus nerve accelerate SA discharge rate, increasing rate of contraction

Athlete's heart enlarges

Output of hormones promoted by sympathetic stimulation

Blood flow diminishes in kidneys

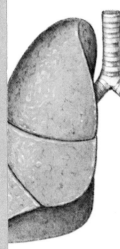

...gs respond to greater ...d for oxygen and the build-up ...arbon dioxide by increasing ...th of breathing

...Liver receives less blood

Muscles require more oxygen

risk factor. This is partly because everyone reacts differently to life's events. One person falls apart under the same circumstances that leave another unruffled. Stress is not a twentieth-century phenomenon. Eighteenth-century English physician John Hunter, whose stress threshold was apparently low, once described his life as being "in the hands of any rascal who chooses to annoy and tease me." Already suffering from heart disease, Hunter later died from the affliction.

Stress is almost inescapable in modern society. Wilhelm Raab, Professor Emeritus of Medicine at the University of Vermont believes that daily emotional strains "stimulate . . . our brain to bombard the cardiovascular system with oxygen-wasting hormones and chemicals." It is no wonder, he says, that a heart "already overburdened by narrowed coronary arteries and constant hypertension may suddenly find itself too short of fuel to sustain its own pumping needs."

Although such an endless variety of tensions grates on our nerves, stress is not always a negative experience. Hans Selye, a leading authority, defines stress as the nonspecific response of the body to any demand made on it, be it pleasant or unpleasant. Extreme joy, then, can be as stressful as deep despair.

Some scientists believe that a certain amount of stress may be necessary. "It's the high degree of stress that many can't cope with," explains Richard Winter, chairman of the Executive Health Examiners Group, health care specialists that serve more than 800 organizations around the world. "Competitive businessmen and women need to undergo some stress. A certain amount is essential. But it must be handled with keen self-understanding, and some executives lack it or can't employ it."

When confronted with a highly stressful condition, mind and body function together in a cyclical pattern called the fight-or-flight response, a primordial inheritance shared by all vertebrates. The system girds itself to meet the demands of a stressful situation by causing blood pressure, heartbeat and the rate of respiration to soar. This accomplished, the body returns to a state of rest and equilibrium.

Some experts believe stress has become so relentless in modern society that the body is never permitted to return to its normal relaxed state. The large amounts of adrenalin and noradrenalin that pour into the blood stream during fight-or-flight cause the cells of the heart muscle to burn oxygen at a very high rate, quickly depleting the heart's oxygen supply. The resulting oxygen deficiency could lead to a heart attack in a person with coronary heart disease.

Recent studies have strengthened the statistical link between stress and heart disease. In a study of 150 middle-aged men, Swedish scientists found that those who experienced a high degree of psychological stress were six times more likely to develop coronary heart disease within five years than those who reported relatively little stress. Another study showed that individuals over the age of forty-five whose spouses die have a very high rate of heart attack during the first six months alone.

Hoping to identify the effects of stress in people with the same genetic inheritance, Norwegian researchers studied a large number of identical twins. The scientists discovered that the twins who had suffered heart attacks had worked much harder than their healthy siblings.

Stress may also be the key to sudden deaths of people with no known history of heart disease. In one of the largest studies of stress and heart attacks, a group of Boston doctors examined 117 patients who had been revived after suffering serious heart attacks. More than 20 percent of the patients had experienced severe emotional distress during the twenty-four hours preceding the attack. Although the majority showed no sign of heart disease, the doctors believed they had suffered previous damage that weakened the heart.

In many cases, sudden death is caused by ventricular fibrillation, severe arrhythmia of the heart muscle. Scientists know that a certain clus-

Signaling feverishly, brokers trade commodity futures at the Chicago Mercantile Exchange. Intense competition may bring on heart disease in the coronary-prone Type A personality.

ter of nerves in the base of the brain regulates changes in heart rate during stress. Experiments have shown that laboratory animals under stress are highly susceptible to fibrillation. If the brain cell cluster in these animals is destroyed, they do not experience the fatal heart irregularity when exposed to stressful conditions. Scientists are working to develop a drug for humans which would soften the impact of stress by dampening electrical impulses sent from this brain center.

Type A Behavior

Although stress affects everyone from time to time, people with a certain type of personality may be more likely to lead stress-filled lives. Ray H. Rosenman and Meyer Friedman, cardiologists at Mount Zion Hospital in San Francisco, first described the "Type A" personality in 1959. Wondering whether the standard medical advice to cut cholesterol, stop smoking and exercise regularly was really helping their patients, the doctors began searching for another explanation for coronary heart disease. They noticed that most of their patients were achievement-oriented, had a strong competitive drive, were very impatient and became hostile at the slightest provocation. The doctors concluded that these personality traits predisposed the patients toward coronary heart disease. Laboratory experiments with animals convinced Rosenman and Friedman that Type A behavior prompted the brain to stimulate the production of cholesterol-raising hormones, which, in turn, could hasten the development of atherosclerosis.

The doctors have impressive statistics to support their theory. Studies of thirty-five hundred middle-aged men showed that long-term Type A behavior was the best predictor of coronary heart disease. Such men were almost three times more likely than patient, noncompetitive Type B men to develop heart disease within ten years.

The Type A theory has recently gained broad acceptance in the medical community. In an on-going study sponsored by the National Institutes of Health, researchers are studying Type A heart attack victims participating in a program to change their behavior. According to Friedman, those who have participated in group therapy to

subdue their Type A characteristics seem to have a lower rate of second heart attacks than those who do not receive any therapy.

Another study suggesting that personality plays a role in heart disease and other serious illnesses was conducted by researchers at Johns Hopkins University. For three decades, they followed 1,337 medical students who had graduated from the university in 1948. The doctors chose forty-five students at random and divided them into three categories based on psychological traits. The "alphas" were stable, even-tempered and deliberate. "Betas" were adaptable, spontaneous and bright. The "gammas" were a complicated group, temperamentally shifting between wariness and impulsive behavior.

After examining the subjects' records for serious illnesses, the researchers found striking differences in the health of the three groups. The intense, moody gammas had the worst medical history. Seventy-seven percent of the gammas developed a major illness, including heart disease, after reaching middle age. One member of the research team believes temperament might have been the most important factor in the development of the gammas' illnesses.

While the impact of stress on the mind and emotions has been shown to contribute to coronary heart disease, several studies indicate that grief caused by loneliness or the absence of loving companionship can also lead to physical illness. One researcher found that the death rate from coronary heart disease is much higher among single people of both sexes, all ages and all races than for those who are married.

Although personality studies such as these may seem overly simplistic, they show the zeal with which scientists are scouring every aspect of twentieth-century life in search of clues to the heart disease puzzle. Many doctors believe they can no longer ignore the possibility that the mind and the emotions somehow nourish or endanger the heart. More and more, they are looking for a combination of factors, some purely physiological, others entangled in the more nebulous realms of emotions or mind. Or perhaps the key to the heart's vulnerability lies in some element not yet explored or even imagined.

Chapter 5

Disorders of the Heart

The heart is a faithful pump. Moving blood, it feeds the organs that give the body life. Cripple the pump and damage ripples through the system. The lungs flood, the kidneys grow slack, the liver fails. A healthy heart unites the body's intricate order. A heart in trouble implies chaos.

Heart disease can blight all parts of the organ. It can be valvular, electrical or vascular in nature. Infection can spawn it, as can heredity. Some people have the misfortune to be born with malformed hearts. But the most prevalent form of heart disease attacks the organ's muscular essence. It is commonly known as heart attack.

An oft-uttered but seldom defined term, heart attack means death of a portion of heart muscle, a condition described medically as myocardial infarction. Eighty percent of all heart attacks derive from cardiovascular disease, primarily from diseased coronary arteries. If, over time, these two essential conduits fill with fatty substances, heart attack looms. While most organs use about a quarter of the blood supplied them, the heart uses 80 percent. Many organs can survive for hours without a fresh dose of oxygen, but the heart will die if denied its supply for much longer than half an hour.

As the heart contracts it compresses the coronary arteries and slows the passage of blood to a trickle. When the heart relaxes the flow resumes, nourishing cardiac tissue with blood. It is thus a sign of sound biological design that the heart normally relaxes for about 60 percent of its cycle of systole and diastole. An inefficient heart that must constantly accelerate its beat spends less time in heart-nourishing relaxation.

Coronary heart disease almost always results from arteriosclerosis, hardening of the arteries. Scientists believe a heavy veneer of fat builds along the interior of vessel walls in places where the smooth arterial lining has been torn or in-

The pulse proves an age-old measure as revealed by The Doctor's Visit, *painted by the seventeenth-century Dutch master Frans van Mieris the Elder. Today, physicians still rely on this simple guide to diagnosis.*

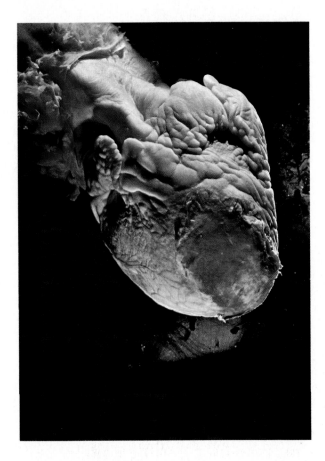

jured. The deposits of fat, known as plaques, calcify into a chalky substance, and the healthy elastic wall changes into dead and unresponsive scar tissue. As this occurs, the artery grows brittle and less resilient, losing its ability to absorb the surges of blood routinely pumped by the heart.

The continuing pulsations of blood can pound the brittle artery out of shape. A bulge known as an aneurysm forms and grows, perhaps one day to burst. A ruptured aneurysm in the abdomen causes shock. In the aorta it is usually fatal.

The plaques that form in hardened arteries can also act as magnets for blood platelets, the cellular components involved in blood coagulation. The platelets stick to plaques, growing into blood clots called thrombi. As the blood clot grows larger, it reduces blood flow through the artery. A clot in the heart can also break free from the heart wall and be carried down the blood stream. This free-flowing blood clot may ultimately lodge in a vital artery, causing an embolism. What makes emboli so deadly is the suddenness with which they strike. They usually deny the affected artery the time it would need to develop additional, bypassing vessels. If an embolism is not treated, the tissue fed by the artery dies from lack of blood flow.

Warnings of Attack

Although frequently sudden, a heart attack does not always come without warning. Often accompanying the build-up of fatty deposits in coronary arteries is a pain called angina pectoris. Felt in the limbs as a stab of pain or random twinge, angina pectoris can culminate in a crushing, vise-like sensation in the chest. The discomfort rarely lasts more than a few minutes and is usually brought on by exercise, emotional stress or heavy eating. While it is not a heart attack, the pain of angina signals the gradual choking off of blood flow to the heart.

Blockage of either of the two major coronary arteries shuts off blood flow to some part of the left ventricle, the heart's workhorse chamber. During a severe attack the heart may pump just enough blood to keep the body alive. The lungs fill with fluid. The kidneys cannot clear the blood stream of waste. The victim may be confused because his brain is not receiving enough oxygen. These are symptoms of shock. Recently, doctors have devised ways to insert catheters into the heart to monitor pressure and guide therapy. As a result, more heart attack victims now survive the initial trauma of shock.

After a heart attack, white blood cells swarm to the damaged area to break down the dead tissue. Scar tissue replaces the infarcted, or dead, area in a process which takes about eight weeks. Scar tissue, though durable, signals the absence of muscle. Since it is stiff and lacks elasticity, scar tissue removes forever a part of the heart's capacity to contract. The left ventricle, however, can lose as much as a quarter of its muscle and still function as an effective pump. That is the heart's enormous margin of safety.

Disease of the heart muscle takes the generic name cardiomyopathy. Disease that directly alters the structure or function of heart muscle is

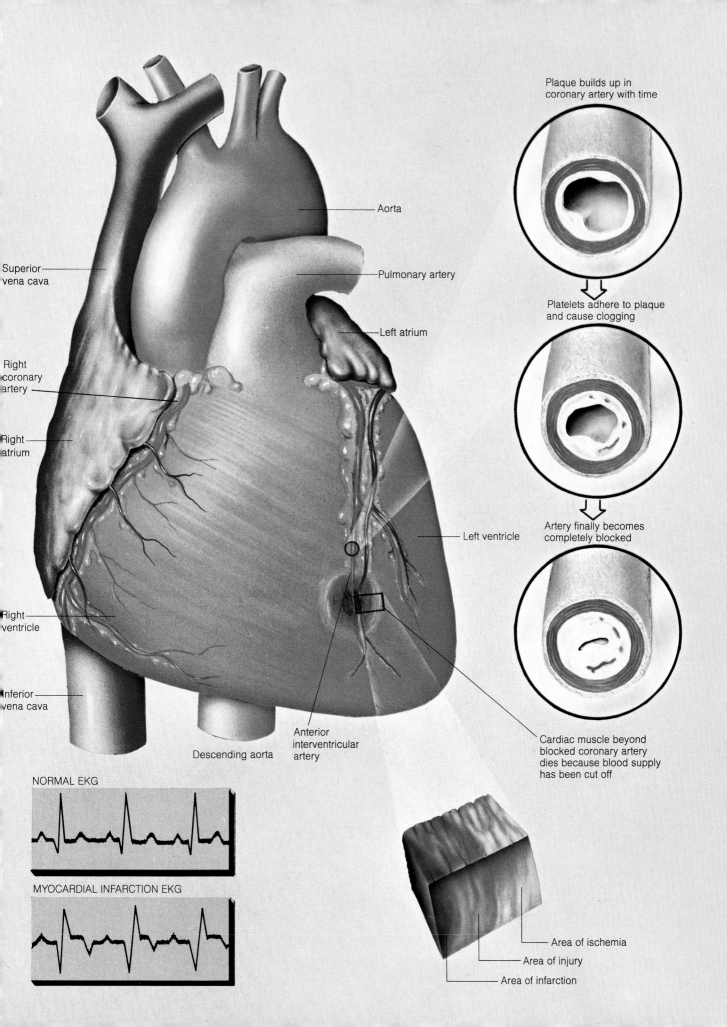

Aorta

Pulmonary artery

Left atrium

Left ventricle

Superior
vena cava

Right
coronary
artery

Right
atrium

Right
ventricle

Inferior
vena cava

Descending aorta

Anterior
interventricular
artery

Plaque builds up in
coronary artery with time

Platelets adhere to plaque
and cause clogging

Artery finally becomes
completely blocked

Cardiac muscle beyond
blocked coronary artery
dies because blood supply
has been cut off

NORMAL EKG

MYOCARDIAL INFARCTION EKG

Area of ischemia

Area of injury

Area of infarction

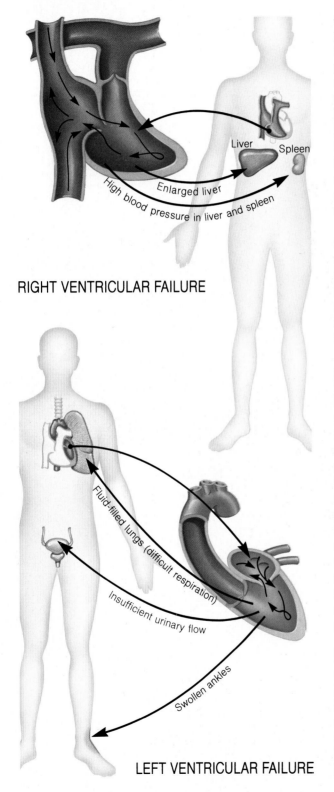

RIGHT VENTRICULAR FAILURE

LEFT VENTRICULAR FAILURE

called primary cardiomyopathy. It can take two principal forms — hypertrophic or congestive. In the hypertrophic variety, the muscle fibers composing the bulk of the heart wall begin to thicken. Sometimes, too, the septum swells, impeding the flow of blood from the left ventricle to the body. The thickened wall can also distort a leaflet of the mitral valve, causing it to leak. Swelling of the septum is believed to be hereditary. Symptoms of this ailment include shortness of breath, dizziness and heart murmur. Cardiac arrhythmia, malfunction of the heart's electrical system, can also develop.

In congestive cardiomyopathy, which is more common than the other form, the heart cavity enlarges. The myocardium tends to degenerate, and fibrous tissue supplants healthy muscle. As blood flow slackens through an enlarged heart, the risk of clotting rises. Clots, in time, can break free from the muscle wall and flush into the systemic or pulmonary circulations.

When the heart is abnormally weakened, congestive heart failure can result. Either or both of the ventricles, the heart's pumping chambers, fail to empty fully during systole. Cardiac output decreases while pressure builds simultaneously in the atria, the chambers that supply the ventricles with blood. In left ventricular failure, the extra pressure in the left atrium forces blood back into the pulmonary veins, which bring fresh blood from the lungs. These vessels then congest, impairing respiration. If the right ventricle fails, blood backs into the large veins feeding the right atrium. The veins distend and circulatory congestion occurs in the vital organs. The kidneys lose their ability to excrete sodium, forcing the body to retain more fluid than normal. Tissues become clogged with chemical wastes. This condition is marked by a pronounced swelling of the limbs.

Bacterial and viral ailments also afflict the heart. A bacterial infection called endocarditis can attack and inflame the inner lining of the heart. Wartlike growths appear, usually clustering on heart valves. Formed of bacteria, blood cells and protein, the growths can break off and clog peripheral arteries. Bacteria contaminate the blood stream, spreading infection. In severe cases heart valve damage can result.

Sir William Osler

Pursuing the Heart's Subtle Foes

Egerton Yorrick Davis, a little-known figure in Victorian medicine, was frequently confused with a distinguished physician of his time, Sir William Osler. They had the same bright, intense eyes, the same drooping mustache, the same commanding air.

It could be said that theirs was a family resemblance, for Davis was the child of Osler's mind, a fictional character whose name and nature Osler donned when he did not want to be recognized. Osler had become a popular subject with the press. To rid himself of reporters he would assert, "My name is Davis — E. Y. Davis of Caughnawauga." The playful Davis also helped bolster Osler through the emotional dark moments he experienced when diagnosing patients with heart ailments that were incurable.

Osler was the first physician to recognize endocarditis and to trace its origin to an often harmless bacterium. Usually fatal, endocarditis preyed on weakened hearts, those with valves damaged by rheumatic fever or congenital defects. It crippled the heart by encrusting the valves with large growths that impeded the flow of blood. The growths also presented another danger. They could easily crumble and become lodged in the arteries.

The linking of bacteria to disease was a relatively modern idea. Louis Pasteur's theories attributing disease to specific microorganisms had only recently gained acceptance. Osler first recognized the symptoms of endocarditis while working in a pathology laboratory in Montreal. In 1885, he prepared a lecture which brought the disease to the widespread attention of his colleagues. One student who attended the lecture later wrote that he could "scarcely keep his seat, with emotion."

In 1888, Osler was appointed Physician in Chief at the recently founded Johns Hopkins Hospital in Baltimore and head of its medical school. He longed to live in England, however, and when he was offered a position as professor of medicine at Oxford in 1904, he eagerly accepted it. Osler's

studies of endocarditis continued and, in 1908, he reported his new findings.

There were two types of bacterial endocarditis, he observed. The acute form, subject of his 1885 lecture, could kill within weeks. But he had also discovered a more subtle and far more common form of the disease that was also fatal. Often, the patient experienced no discomfort other than a fever of perhaps 100 to 101 degrees. This low-grade fever could last for months, sometimes stretching to a year. Osler sought to alert doctors to the difficulty of this diagnosis.

Although Osler now understood what was killing his patients, he had no way to stop it. Doctors did not learn how to treat endocarditis until the 1940s, when penicillin came into wide use. Large doses of the drug could bring the disease under control and prevent it from striking likely victims.

Endocarditis was only one of Osler's many challenges. A prolific author, he wrote more than 700 books and articles on a wide variety of medical subjects. But the physician was admired as much for his compassion and wit as for his scientific achievements. "I have made mistakes," he once said, "but they have been mistakes of the head, not of the heart."

The pericardium, the membrane surrounding the heart, can also become inflamed. Infected by a virus, it becomes rough and thick. Fluid seeps into the pericardial sac. Pericarditis, the resulting illness, most often occurs in young people. Manifested as pain in the chest or left shoulder, the disease is usually benign.

Pericarditis often appears in conjunction with myocarditis, the inflammation of heart muscle. Heart muscle is vulnerable to almost any blood-borne infectious, toxic or inflammatory disease because its ceaseless labor demands a rich blood supply, roughly 400 quarts a day. But the heart has abundant defenses. Blood vessels and the lymphatic system can efficiently drain away harmful fluids. In many cases, the inflammation is isolated in a small area of heart muscle and no symptoms appear. When a sufficiently broad section of the heart muscle becomes inflamed, however, the disease may prove troublesome. Then myocarditis causes fatigue and can rouse arrhythmia. In extreme cases, the disease can cause ventricular failure.

Murmurs and Leaks

Another ailment stems from rheumatic fever, a disease that often begins innocently as a sore throat or ear infection. Ultimately, it can attack the fine inner workings of the heart. Rheumatic fever is spawned by streptococcal bacteria. The body's immune system responds by manufacturing antibodies, which, in a cruel twist of fate, can attack certain heart tissues. In the case of rheumatic fever, nature's cure can prove worse than the disease. The illness usually preys on the heart valves. It inflames the cusps, forming lesions which in time fuse and narrow the openings of the valves. Robbed of their easy movement, valves can no longer seal off the heart's chambers. With each heartbeat, some blood leaks backward. The former condition is stenosis; the latter, regurgitation.

Stenosis usually affects the valves that do the heaviest work — those on the heart's left side. The mitral valve, linking the left atrium and ventricle, is frequently the most badly damaged. The second most affected is the aortic valve, which joins the left ventricle and aorta.

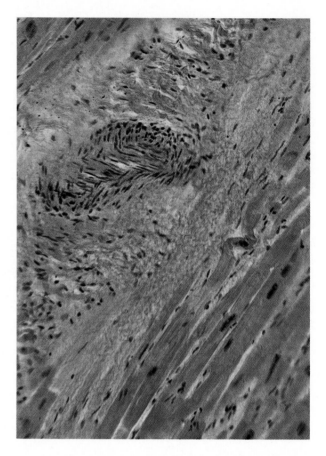

Like a knot in a piece of pine, inflamed tissue breaks the striated grain of heart muscle. Rheumatic fever, which focuses on the valves, also scars and weakens the heart's muscular fabric.

In aortic stenosis, the left ventricle loses the ability to empty itself fully of blood. Internal pressure can rise as high as 350 millimeters of mercury, three times normal. A "nozzle effect" results, as blood under high pressure shoots through the narrowed opening. The gush of blood into the aorta sets up intense vibrations in the artery. This turbulence echoes in the ear of the doctor listening with his stethoscope. What he hears is a heart murmur, an abnormal sound which can have four separate cadences, depending on the phase of the cardiac cycle and the valve affected. Mitral regurgitation and aortic stenosis can be heard during systole. Aortic regurgitation and mitral stenosis are heard during diastole. Each, with its own distinct murmur, announces itself to the knowledgeable ear.

In the case of the aortic valve, the twin scourges of stenosis and regurgitation create a net loss in stroke volume. The left ventricle cannot

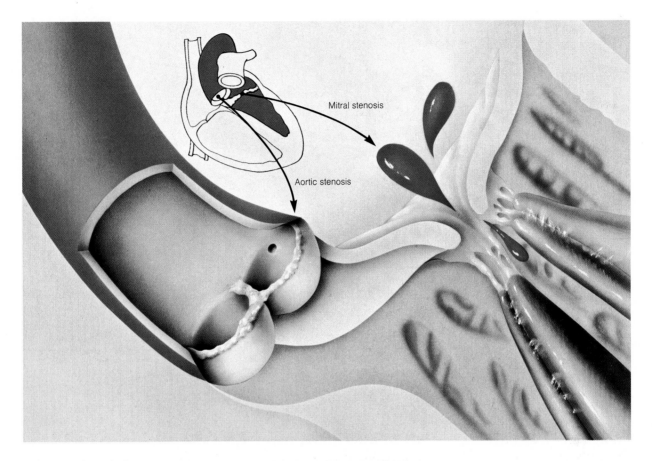

Mitral stenosis

Aortic stenosis

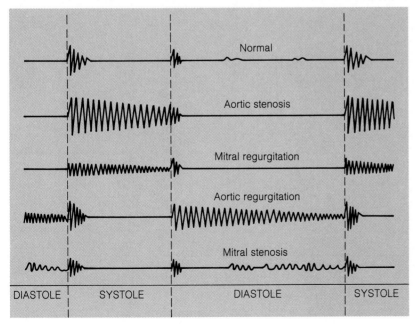

Normal

Aortic stenosis

Mitral regurgitation

Aortic regurgitation

Mitral stenosis

DIASTOLE   SYSTOLE   DIASTOLE   SYSTOLE

Scourge of the working heart, rheumatic fever scars the valves, causing them to harden and fuse. The disease both narrows the valve openings and impairs their ability to seal a chamber tight. Murmurs, the turbulent sound of blood shooting through a narrow opening or sloshing back through a leaky valve, read out, left, on a phonocardiogram, a sounding of the heart in action.

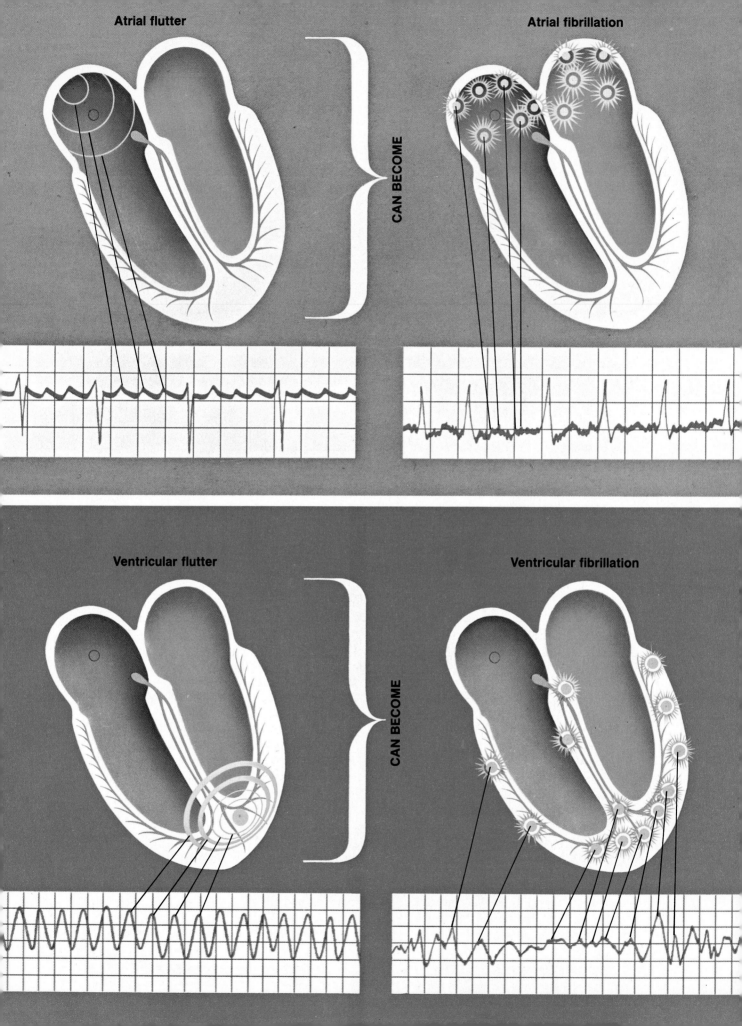

Atrial flutter

Atrial fibrillation

CAN BECOME

Ventricular flutter

Ventricular fibrillation

CAN BECOME

fully empty during systole. In diastole, blood seeps back from the aorta into the left ventricle when it should be traveling in the opposite direction. As the amount of blood pumped to the body drops, the heart does its best to compensate. The left ventricle pumps harder, putting on muscle in the process. It might increase five times its normal size.

The severity of valve disease varies. Some people live for years without experiencing any pain. Others suffer mild discomfort. Over time, however, valve disease tends to worsen and may eventually disable the sufferer. When the disease is severe, the left ventricle cannot pump its normal quota of blood. It begins to depend on the left atrium, leaving the upper chamber to collect and hold blood that would ordinarily flow into the ventricle. Two things then happen. First, higher pressure in the ventricle reduces blood flow through the coronary arteries and to other organs. Second, blood backs up into the pulmonary veins and makes new demands on the lungs. The lungs' lymphatic system responds, expanding to drain off as much as ten times the normal amount of fluid. If the condition does not improve, fluid builds around the alveoli, the air sacs in the lungs. Pulmonary edema, the accumulation of fluid in the lungs, sets in. If severe enough, pulmonary edema can result in death.

Short-Circuiting the Heart

If the surface of the left atrium is sufficiently stretched, the impulses triggered by the pacemaker in the right atrium must travel greater distances to work their magic. This portends a new and related problem — cardiac arrhythmia, the short-circuiting of the heart's electrical system.

A variety of factors can spark abnormal heartbeats. These range from the skewing of the pacemaker's cadence to the delayed conduction or interruption of the electrical signal in its passage through the heart muscle. The last condition is called heart block. It occurs at the AV node, the electrical connection between the atria and ventricles. Heart block is a question of degree. It can be intermittent, in which case every second or third impulse will pass through the AV node. Or it can be complete. In this case, the ventricles

may eventually tire of waiting for an impulse that does not come and begin to contract on their own, usually at a slower rate than the atria. This phenomenon is called "ventricular escape."

Another arrhythmic spark is the ectopic, or premature, beat. This stimulus is generated from a site other than the SA node and is often triggered by ischemia, reduced flow of blood to a patch of heart muscle. The tissue grows anxious, "irritable," impatient, and its cells depolarize on their own initiative. Stimulants, anxiety or excessive fatigue can also kindle ectopic beats. These random impulses pose little danger. They reflect more the stress of the moment, the anxious heart that quite literally can skip a beat. But should ectopic beats come in lengthy sequence, meshing their rhythm with the pacemaker's — or even usurping it — there is cause for concern.

Electrical Frenzies

A flurry of such beats can sometimes build into arrhythmic frenzies called flutter and fibrillation. In atrial flutter, the chambers contract 250 to 350 times a minute but maintain an orderly rhythm. Fibrillation, by comparison, is chaotic. Cells fire at random across the heart, as rapidly as 500 times a minute. The heart muscle ripples like the surface of a still pond broken by a pebble.

Flutter and fibrillation are both thought to arise from a related phenomenon called circus movement. In this situation the heart's electrical impulse chases and catches itself. An electrical process that normally has a beginning and end forges itself instead into a circle.

After cardiac cells contract, they must "rest" before they can fire again. This imposes a physiological ceiling on how fast the heart can beat. Normally, when an impulse runs its course it dies out. It encounters cardiac muscle in a refractory state — cells not yet ready to refire. But in circus movement, reentry is possible. The impulse, having come full circle, links up with cells that have already had their refractory rest. Instead of dying out and making way for its successor, the impulse finds fresh tinder. It rekindles the cycle, speeding the heartbeat and giving rise to flutter.

Circus movement may occur in three ways. First, the path the impulse travels can lengthen, so that by the time the impulse completes its trip it finds cells that have already passed through the refractory period. Second, the impulse can move at a reduced speed. Third, the refractory period can shorten. A number of conditions create these three possibilities. A thickened, dilated heart lengthens the pathway. Ischemic or infarcted heart tissues lose some or all of their ability to conduct impulses. They slow or even divert the electrical impulse from its normal path. Stimulants can also alter the ionic content of heart cells and thereby shorten the refractory time.

If left untreated, flutter can degenerate into the chaos of fibrillation. The trademark of fibrillation is the creation of a chain reaction within the heart. An impulse reaching a refractory "patch" of muscle divides, so anxious is it to bypass this block. The two new stimuli proceed, until they stumble upon another refractory patch. Again they split, producing four impulses where a normally functioning heart would tolerate only one. This multiplying process soon spreads out of control. More impulses create more refractory patches. Ultimately the heart begins to fibrillate.

Fortunately, fibrillation is usually confined to the atria by the fibrous tissue that separates them from the ventricles. A person can endure atrial fibrillation for several years because the atria act only as primers to the vital pumps, the ventricles. The work of the atria normally accounts for about a quarter of the volume of blood pumped to the ventricles. Atrial fibrillation reduces the filling ability of the heart to about 75 percent. But this still falls within the cardiac reserve, the margin of safety designed into the heart. The ventricles can fill themselves.

If the ventricles enter fibrillation, however, the heart loses all power to pump blood. As the ventricle walls ripple ineffectively, the chambers dilate and engorge with blood. As time passes, the volume of blood in the chambers, and the task of moving it, increases. The chaotic contractions of the ventricles, meanwhile, grow more and more feeble. Very rarely will the heart return to its normal rhythm. Without immediate medical treatment, a person experiencing ventricular fibrillation would be fortunate to survive more than a minute and a half. To shock the heart back to its normal rhythm, physicians use an electrical defibrillator. This machine sends an electrical impulse through ventricular muscle fibers, throwing them into a refractory state. This halts the heart's electrical activity for three-to-five seconds. If the procedure is successful, the SA node will begin to fire in an orderly rhythm, and the heart will beat again in its normal fashion.

The Malformed Heart

In the womb, the heart evolves from a hollow tube into a four-chambered pump in only eight weeks. Bulging, twisting, folding, it swells into shape. There is, in the midst of such surging growth, ample room for error. Yet in only one-half of one percent of all American births does a congenital defect arise. Three decades ago many such defects doomed their victims to sedentary lives or to early or sudden death. Today, surgeons can mend postnatal holes, replace valves and rearrange whole sections of the heart.

Nonetheless, the causes of congenital defects remain a clouded corner of medical knowledge. Researchers point to three possibilities. Hereditary error, the transmission of faulty chromosomal information, occurs in a fraction of cases — perhaps 1 or 2 percent. A second source of heart defects is injury to the fetus during the critical days of heart formation. This can take the form of a vitamin deficiency through faulty maternal metabolism or poor diet. It may also occur as a side effect of a well-intended drug gone awry, such as thalidomide. Disease, the third cause of heart defects, wreaks far less havoc than it once did. German measles, rubella, long the scourge of maternal, and thus fetal health, can blind and deform the unborn if the mother contracts it during pregnancy. Today, vaccination tames it. The result in all three of these cases is a malformed heart which either blocks or redirects blood flow. Deadly defects that impede blood flow include pulmonary stenosis, aortic stenosis and coarctation of the aorta.

In pulmonary and aortic stenosis, the valves linking the ventricles with the two major arteries are narrowed. The valve leaflets fuse together and lose their ability to open fully. This blocks the normal passage of blood. The ventricle must

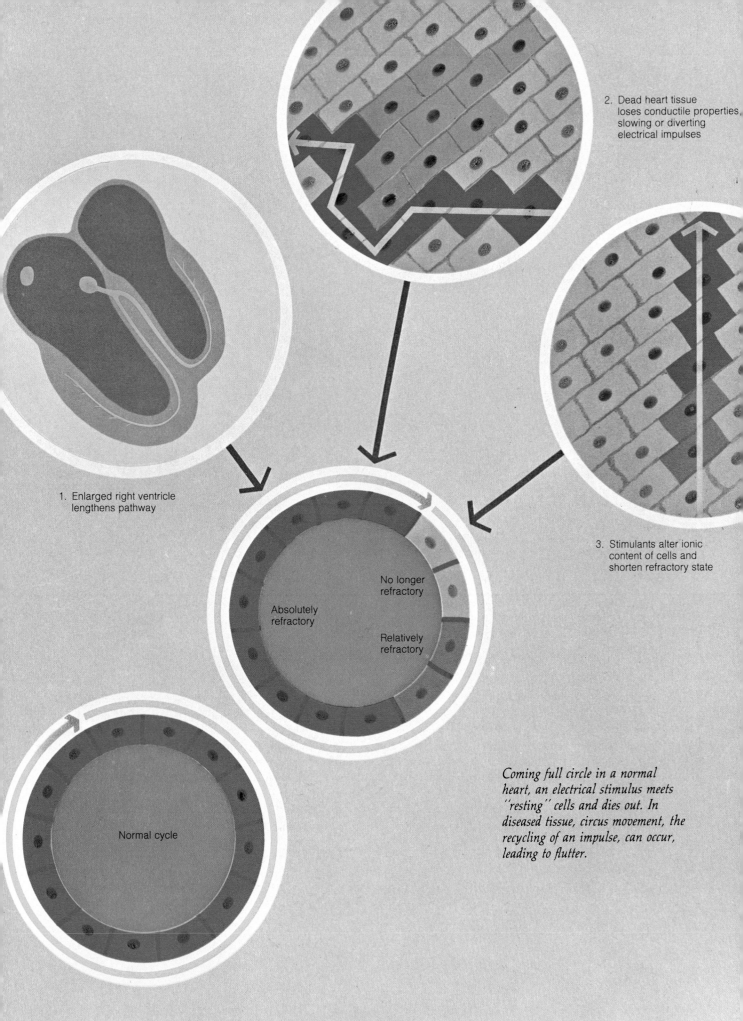

2. Dead heart tissue loses conductile properties, slowing or diverting electrical impulses

1. Enlarged right ventricle lengthens pathway

3. Stimulants alter ionic content of cells and shorten refractory state

No longer refractory

Absolutely refractory

Relatively refractory

Normal cycle

Coming full circle in a normal heart, an electrical stimulus meets "resting" cells and dies out. In diseased tissue, circus movement, the recycling of an impulse, can occur, leading to flutter.

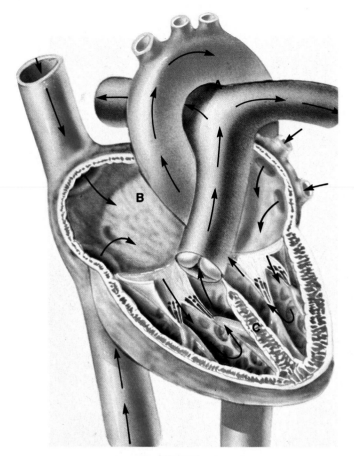

Normal

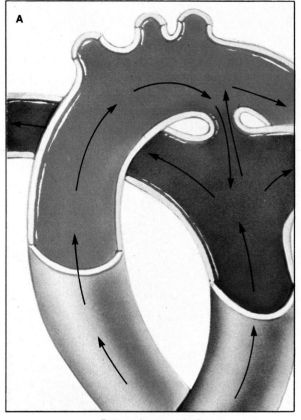

Patent ductus arteriosus

Sabotaging the normal heart's division of labor, many congenital defects link the organ's two halves. At various sites (A, B and C), they permit used blood to taint fresh and force the muscle to work overtime. Patent ductus arteriosus and atrial septal defect (A and B) arise when channels allowing blood to bypass the dormant lungs in the fetus fail to close at birth. Ventricular septal defect (C) occurs when the two ridges that grow together to form the heart's partitioning wall do not fully join.

pump at a higher pressure — perhaps five times normal — to push blood through the blockage. Enlargement of the heart muscle also occurs.

In coarctation of the aorta, the artery mysteriously narrows before birth. This reduces the flow of oxygenated blood to the body. As in stenosis, pressure builds in the heart and the blood backs up. Congestive heart failure can result.

Other congenital defects arise from pathways in the fetal circulatory system that allow most of the blood to bypass the fetus's collapsed lungs. A small hole in the midwall of the fetal heart, the foramen ovale, allows blood to flow from the right atrium to the left, so that it can be pumped to the body by the left ventricle. Another temporary conduit, the ductus arteriosus, drains blood from the pulmonary artery and feeds it to the aorta. At birth the umbilical cord is clamped and cut. The infant must now breathe for itself. The lungs inflate, and the ductus arteriosus constricts,

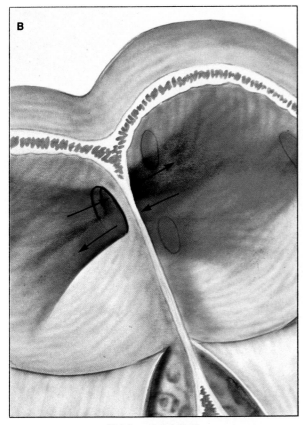

Atrial septal defect

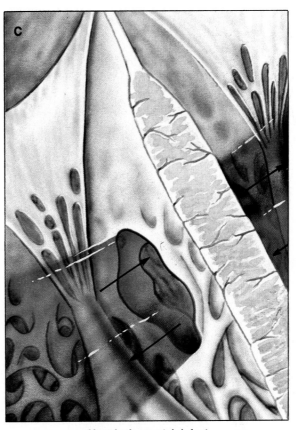

Ventricular septal defect

in time to wither into a thread of ligament. Pressure in the left atrium is sufficient to limit blood flow from right to left atrium. This pressure works the foramen ovale into a flap of tissue that will close and seal in the first year of life.

This, at least, is how it should be. But sometimes the duct and the septal wall fail to close, causing, respectively, patent ductus arteriosus and atrial septal defect. An atrial septal defect permits blood to flow from the left to the right atrium, leading to the latter's enlargement. In patent ductus arteriosus, blood meant for the body travels instead to the lungs. In extreme cases the lungs may receive twice as much blood as the arterial system. With such a disproportion, the left ventricle must work doubly hard. Hypertrophy and dilation of the ventricle occur, eventually leading to heart failure.

Ventricular septal defect, a hole in the wall between the ventricles, mimics the symptoms of

Helen Taussig

Guardian of Tiny Hearts

In the 1930s, doctors in the pediatrics division of Johns Hopkins Hospital called the short-lived, startlingly blue-skinned babies their "crossword puzzles." When Helen Taussig, a Johns Hopkins heart specialist, viewed the autopsies of such children, she suspected that they had died from a lack of oxygen. The children were born with a heart defect that hindered some of the body's mechanisms for oxygenating blood. An opening in the wall between the ventricles allowed oxygenated and unoxygenated blood to mingle. And the valve of the pulmonary artery, the major path from heart to lungs, was narrowed.

Taussig found clues to the blue babies' misery in the fetal circulatory system. It had special paths to spare blood an unnecessary trip through the unused lungs of the fetus. One of the pathways — the ductus arteriosus — connected the pulmonary artery to the aorta, enabling some blood to bypass the lungs and go immediately to the body. Once the infant began breathing, these openings normally closed.

But when the ductus of blue babies began to close, the children's blue coloring intensified. Taussig realized that these children still needed the ductus, but for the reverse pur-

pose. The connection between the ductus and the pulmonary artery allowed some blood to make an extra trip through the lungs, increasing the amount of oxygenated blood in the body. The normal closing of the ductus became a deadly process in blue babies by sealing off a path to the lungs.

Taussig was searching for a solution when a Boston doctor captured her attention. He had daringly entered a young girl's heart to seal off an improperly closed ductus. If a ductus could be tied off, Taussig reasoned, perhaps one could be built. In 1940, she went to Boston to discuss her idea with the doc-

tor but found "he wasn't in the least interested" in the possibility of building one. "Closing a ductus was the great thing."

Then, Taussig learned that a nationally known vascular surgeon, Alfred Blalock, was coming to Johns Hopkins. She kept a watchful eye on his progress. After Blalock had successfully tied off a ductus, Taussig approached him. "I stand in awe . . . of your surgical skill," she told him, "but the really great day will come when you build me a ductus for a child who is dying because too little blood is going to the lungs."

"When that day comes," Blalock replied, "this will seem like child's play." Accepting her challenge, he experimented on hundreds of dogs. Finally, he announced he was ready to try the operation. By late 1944, they had their first patient.

The concept behind the operation was simple but the results were spectacular. The doctors chose one of the major arteries stemming from the aortic arch, turned it toward the heart and joined it to the pulmonary artery. This procedure sent some of the blood back to the lungs. "I walked to the head of the table," Taussig recalled of an operation on a young boy, "and there he was with bright pink cheeks and very red lips!"

patent ductus arteriosus, though it can often prove to be a more serious defect. This depends on the size of the opening. The defect permits fresh blood in the left ventricle to mingle with used blood in the opposite chamber. Pressure between the two ventricles levels off, impairing the pumping power of each chamber. Though grave, this defect, like others, occurs rarely.

Tetralogy of Fallot, named for the French physician who first described the defect in 1888, is one of the most involved of all congenital malformations. It is really the combination of four defects. Prime among these are ventricular septal defect and pulmonary stenosis. These, in turn, create two more problems. The muscle walls of the right ventricle thicken, and blood flows from both ventricles into the aorta.

Tetralogy of Fallot, transposition of the great arteries and hypoplastic left-heart syndrome result in cyanosis, the circulation of blood that has been denied passage through the lungs. Cyanosis appears as a bluish tint in the skin, and it is from this condition that the term ''blue baby'' derives.

Transposition of the great arteries means that the pulmonary and aortic arteries arise from the wrong sides of the heart. The aorta branches from the right side; the pulmonary artery, from the left. The aorta thus receives venous blood and forces it back into a system that cries for oxygen. The pulmonary artery recycles fresh blood to the lungs from which it just came. This defect spells doom if surgery does not follow soon after birth.

Hypoplastic left-heart syndrome refers to the underdevelopment or absence of structures on that side of the heart. This condition does not surface until birth. It is then that the infant, beginning to breathe, needs the left ventricle to receive and pump fresh blood to the body. With the capacity of the left ventricle greatly reduced, often even surgery cannot save the child.

Today, fate is far less a factor in congenital heart disease. What nature omitted medical science is often able to restore. From the healing of cardiac disorders — congenital and acquired — man's understanding of the heart grows. Therein lies the hope that heart disease will one day be rendered a shadow of its present self.

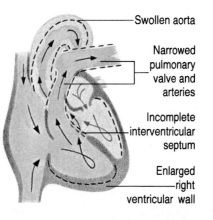

- Swollen aorta
- Narrowed pulmonary valve and arteries
- Incomplete interventricular septum
- Enlarged right ventricular wall

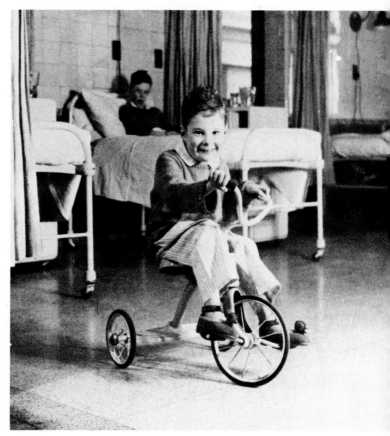

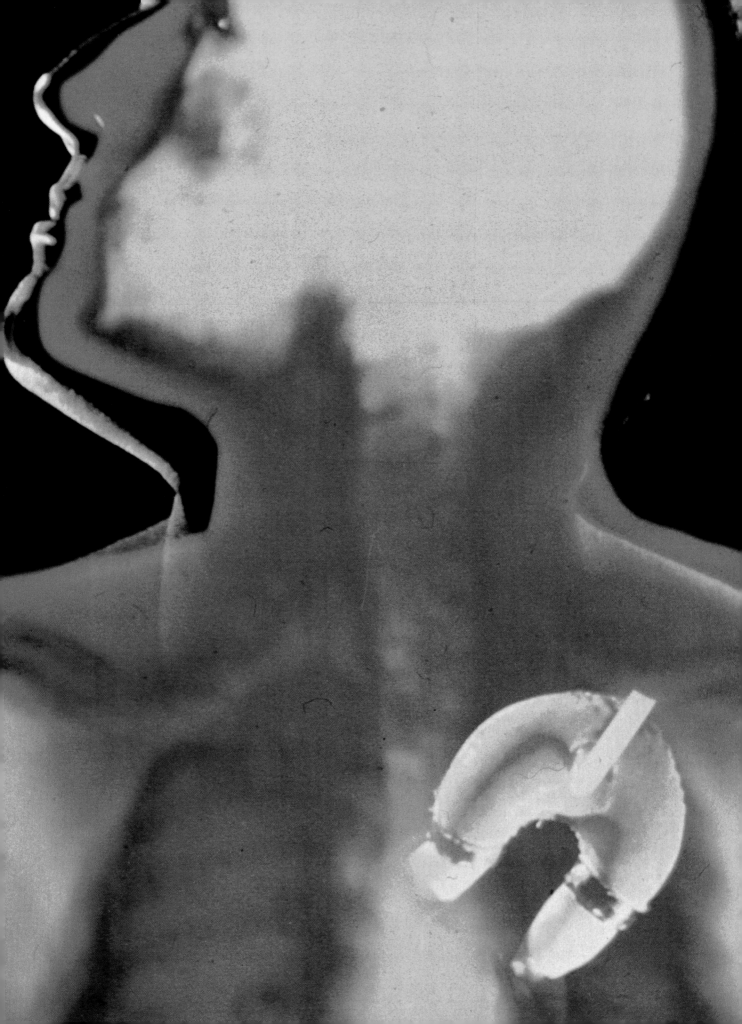

Chapter 6

Modern Miracles

"The heart alone, of all viscera," proclaimed Aristotle, "cannot withstand injury." A wounded heart, until very recently, meant almost certain death. And for most of medical history, since no surgeon dared invade the heart, an abnormal heart also frequently meant death — a mysterious, early death, from causes unseen and unsuspected.

Judging from its position in the chest — encased in the ribs and protected front and back by the sternum and the spinal column — Nature never intended the living heart to be seen, much less sliced open, sutured and restored. But in the late 1800s, as surgical techniques improved and medicine began the transition into modern science, the possibility that surgeons might invade the heart lurked, barely acknowledged, on the fringe of acceptable medicine.

To open the heart would be an errand of mercy. In 1873, a British physician successfully plucked a two-inch-long needle from the heart muscle of a wounded man. In the early 1880s, however, German surgeon and professor of medicine Albert Christian Theodor Billroth issued a stern warning against opening the human heart. "Any surgeon who would attempt an operation on the heart should lose the respect of his colleagues," Billroth declared. The heart after all was surgical terra incognita, blanketed by a fog of mystery and misconception. A decade later, British surgeon and medical historian Stephen Paget echoed Billroth's sentiments when he wrote, "Surgery of the heart has probably reached the limits set by Nature to all surgery; no new method and no new discovery can overcome the natural difficulties that attend a wound of the heart." The same year that Paget set the boundaries for heart surgery, a German physician, Ludwig Rehn, crossed them.

On September 8, 1896, a dying German soldier was carried into a Frankfurt hospital. Seeing that

Man's medical inventiveness has reached inside the chest and touched the human heart. For minutes, hours or, in some cases, years, physicians can make metal, plastic and electricity do the work of muscle, fiber and nerve. Devices like the auxiliary ventricle can temporarily ease the heart's workload and give the heart the chance to heal itself.

The development of effective anesthetics in the mid-1800s began a
medical revolution and set surgery
on a path that would eventually lead
to the heart. A knowledge of the
effects of ether became a vital part
of the surgeon's education, above.
Scientists around the world soon
invented an array of devices, such
as the Dubois chloroform inhaler,
right, to make the surgical use of
anesthetics safer.

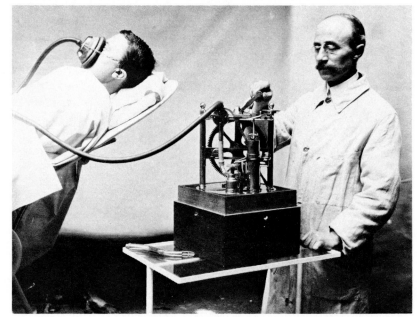

a knife had penetrated the soldier's heart, a doctor put an ice pack on the man's chest, gave him a shot of morphine and left him for dead. The next day, Rehn examined the soldier and decided that nearly inevitable death by surgery was preferable to certain death by delay. After anesthetizing the patient, Rehn opened the chest, cut through the pericardium and reached into the chest cavity. He lifted the apex of the heart and held it for a few moments, throbbing in his hand. Three quick sutures stopped the bleeding, and Rehn sewed up the chest. His patient recovered completely.

Rehn had taken the first steps into a new medical era, but the idea of cutting open a heart was so overwhelming, the dangers so great, that few surgeons dared to follow his lead. More than fifty years would pass before heart surgery would become an accepted, reliable form of treatment. During that time, developments in other areas of medicine would provide the tools surgeons needed to safely enter the living heart.

Anesthetics and Antiseptics

Two discoveries of the mid-1800s were of crucial importance to heart surgery, and surgery in general: antiseptics and anesthetics. The work of Hungarian physician Ignaz Semmelweis, who first recognized that unclean conditions in hospital wards led to infections, and the insights of the French scientific genius Louis Pasteur, who proved the existence and deadly power of bacteria, helped pave the way for the work of Joseph Lister, father of modern antiseptic surgery. The British surgeon brought sterilization and antiseptics into the surgical theater. Lister cleaned wounds with carbolic acid, mixed the acid in a steam sprayer to soak the air in the operating room and commanded his junior surgeons to sterilize their surgical instruments. Lister's innovations reduced the postoperative infections that so often followed even successful operations.

During the same period, two doctors introduced modern surgical anesthetics. Boston dentist William Morton successfully demonstrated ether's anesthetic properties in 1846. The news spread around the world and began a surgical revolution literally within days. In 1847, James Simpson, an English obstetrician, first used chloroform to help ease the pain of women in childbirth. Simpson's discovery initially met resistance but was finally accepted after Queen Victoria asked for chloroform to be administered while she gave birth.

The early 1900s saw several other vital medical discoveries that helped open the door to the heart. In 1917, British physician Ivan Magill invented an endotracheal tube that allowed members of a surgical team to administer anesthetics safely. The tube also kept the patient's lungs inflating and deflating efficiently during long operations. Safe blood transfusions were made possible by the discovery of blood types and the development of methods to store blood plasma. Finally, the discovery of penicillin and other antibiotics helped to control bacterial infections.

Exploring the Heart

Despite these advances, most surgeons still hesitated to operate on the heart. Until the 1930s, cardiology was a barely recognized specialization in medicine, and what doctors could not diagnose they could seldom cure. The heart's behavior — its electrical and chemical properties, its frailties and its quirks — was not yet clearly understood. Using X-rays and fluoroscopes, doctors could look inside the chest and see the heart. But they could not probe the organ's inner workings until a young German surgeon, Werner Forssmann, showed the way.

Seeking a method of injecting drugs directly into the heart, Forssmann threaded a thin tube known as a catheter through his veins and into his heart. Later, he used the catheter to inject opaque dye into his heart in an attempt to outline the organ's chambers on X-ray photographs. Although the photographs were poor, the procedure was sound. Using Forssmann's techniques, scientists developed angiocardiography — the photographic exploration of the heart and blood vessels with X-rays and contrast dyes.

Two American cardiologists, André Cournand and D. W. Richards spent ten years exploring the potential of the catheter. In 1941, after many experiments on animals, Cournand felt confident enough to perform the first cardiac catheterization on a human patient. At Bellevue Hospital in

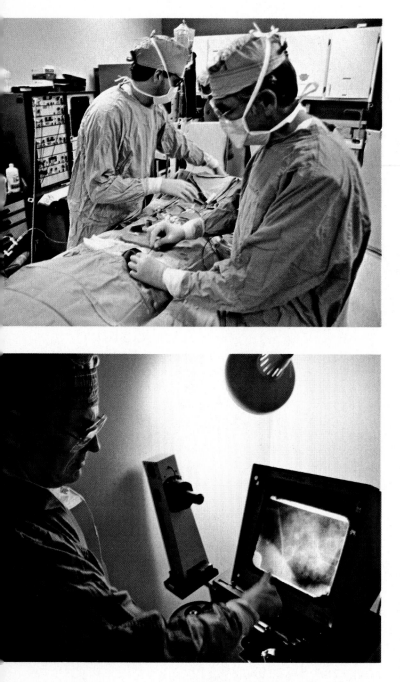

Threading a catheter through a blood vessel in the groin, James Bacos, chairman of cardiology at the Washington Hospital Center in Washington, D.C., prepares to explore the patient's heart.

Modern diagnostic tools such as catheters and X-rays enable doctors to venture inside the chest and return with an angiocardiogram, an invaluable, spectral image of the world inside the heart.

New York City, Cournand successfully probed the heart of a patient suffering from severe hypertension. Cournand's experiment proved that patients could physically and psychologically endure catheterization long enough for cardiologists to explore the heart. Using the methods developed by Cournand and Richards, doctors gained diagnostic information about the heart that could be obtained no other way. Catheterization enabled doctors to measure the flow of blood through the heart and lungs, the volume and pressure of blood in the heart, the pressure of blood flowing through a heart valve and the oxygen content of blood in the heart and major vessels. Catheters could also be used to detect holes in the walls of the heart and congenital abnormalities in the pulmonary artery and aorta.

Throughout the forties and fifties, cardiologists improved the techniques of catheterization and angiocardiography. The invention of an image intensifier for X-rays in the early 1950s gave cardiologists even sharper images of the heart's inner workings. In 1958, Mason Sones, a cardiologist at the Cleveland Clinic, developed coronary angiography, affording doctors their first good look at the arteries that nourish the heart. Sones made repeated attempts at outlining the coronary arteries by injecting contrast dye into the base of the aorta, where the arteries originate. On one of his attempts, he carefully threaded a catheter to one of the small pockets of blood above the cusps of the aortic valve, just outside a coronary artery. When he injected the dye, he was amazed to see the right coronary artery appear on the fluoroscope. The tip of his catheter had slipped into the opening and aimed the dye directly into the artery. His accident proved what some doctors had believed impossible — that contrast dye could be injected into the coronary arteries without disrupting the heart's blood supply. Sones began filming fluoroscopic images of the coronary arteries, providing the first clear views of the blood vessels so often the cause of heart attacks.

Today, cardiologists are experimenting with inflatable balloons at the ends of catheters to pry open constricted coronary arteries. To find the most effective antiarrhythmic drugs, cardiologists are using catheters tipped with electrodes to

Werner Forssmann

Voyager to the Heart

While he was a university student in the early 1920s, Werner Forssmann had seen an engraving on the cover of an old French physiology book showing a man holding rubber tubing inserted in a horse's jugular vein. The tube extended down the animal's neck into its heart. The picture was a primitive but powerful image that would remain in the young man's mind for several years. When he became an intern in a small hospital outside Berlin, Forssmann suggested to his supervisors that such a procedure would yield valuable information about the heart. Surely, he argued, it could be safely performed on man.

His supervisors disagreed. They forbade his testing the procedure on a patient. Determined, Forssmann offered an option. "I'll experiment on myself," he declared. He was swiftly refused. Forssmann was so convinced he was right that he decided to try the experiment in secret. He thought a vein in the arm would offer a safer path to the heart than one in the neck. Assisted by another doctor, Forssmann anesthetized the crook of his left arm. He made an incision in his skin, opened a vein and pushed in a catheter, a slender rubber tube. The doctor helped push about a foot of tubing up

Forssmann's arm, then lost his nerve. He quit, protesting that the experiment was too dangerous. Forssmann had no choice but to withdraw the tube from his arm and discontinue the experiment.

In 1929, on a quiet summer afternoon, Forssmann tried the procedure again. He anesthetized his left elbow, opened the vein and pushed the catheter one foot into his arm. He then called a nurse. Hesitantly, she guided him to the fluoroscope and held up a mirror so that Forssmann could see the machine's shadowy image of his heart. Watching the mirror, he inched the tube through his vein. When the catheter extended twenty-five-and-a-half inches, it had entered his heart. Forssmann went to the X-ray room, insisting a picture be taken to prove the tube had safely entered

his heart. The technician ran out of the room to alert one of Forssmann's colleagues. The frantic doctor dashed in and demanded to know what Forssmann was doing. "He was so desperate he almost tried to pull the catheter out of my arm," Forssmann recalled. "I had to give him a few kicks on the shin to calm him down."

Forssmann attempted the experiment eight times during the next two years. He even injected an opaque dye into his heart so that it would X-ray more clearly. But he met with so much ridicule from his colleagues that he finally abandoned the experiments in catheterization and concentrated on surgery.

Twenty-seven years after his experiment, Forssmann's contribution to the development of cardiac catheterization was finally recognized. In 1956, he was jointly awarded the Nobel Prize for Medicine with American cardiologists André Cournand and D.W. Richards. Forssmann was quietly working as a country doctor in the West German town of Bad Kreuznach when he received word of the honor. The sudden success left him stunned. He felt, remembering with pride, "like a village pastor who is suddenly informed that he has been made a cardinal."

set off abnormal heart rhythms while patients are in the safety of the laboratory. In this way doctors hope to forestall a potentially deadly attack of heart block or ventricular arrhythmia outside the hospital. Still other researchers have used the catheter to inject clot-dissolving enzymes directly into a patient's coronary arteries immediately after a heart attack. This procedure is designed to keep the arteries clear and prevent the crippling damage to heart muscle that regularly follows the obstruction of a coronary artery.

A routine examination by a cardiologist often includes angiocardiography and catheterization, but it begins with less exotic tests. Generally, the doctor will take one or more X-rays to determine the size and shape of the heart. He then uses the electrocardiograph to record the heart's electrical activity. If these tests reveal evidence of a serious heart problem — a defective valve, perhaps, or evidence of a recent heart attack — the cardiologist might then perform a catheterization. A typical catheterization includes blood samples, readings of the oxygen and pressure levels inside the chambers of the heart and angiograms of the heart and major arteries. However, since the procedure is costly — about $2,000 — and carries a slight risk to the patient, the cardiologist might first use a number of recently developed tools that can explore the heart without invading it.

A Portrait in Sound

In the last ten years, the echocardiogram has become an indispensable aid in investigating diseases of the heart. Back in the 1940s, three doctors investigating the properties of sonar reported that high-frequency sound waves could be bounced off the internal organs of the body and be recorded. But echocardiography, the sonar exploration of the heart, is a technology of the sixties and seventies. To create echocardiograms, cardiologists place a small sonar probe called a transducer against the wall of the chest. The probe emits extremely high-frequency sound waves. Organs and tissues of different densities reflect the sound waves back to the probe, which transmits them to a recording device.

Motion-mode echocardiography is the most commonly used technique today. In M-mode, a

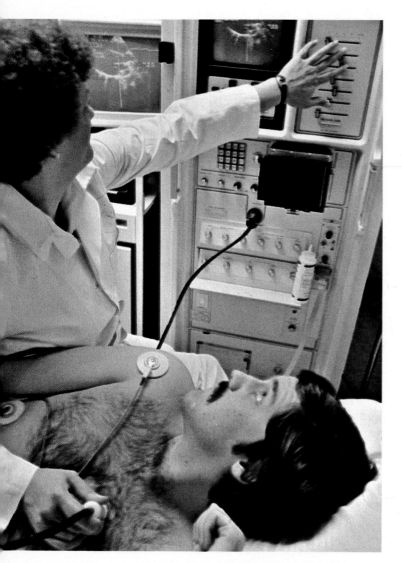

As an echo technician positions a transducer, a patient peers over his shoulder at a two-dimensional, blue-and-white image of his own beating heart. This image, known as an echocardiogram, is reconstructed from the reflections of high-frequency sound waves beamed from the transducer through his chest. The electrodes taped to the patient's ribs and shoulders simultaneously record his electrocardiogram.

transducer sends a single, narrow beam of sound waves through the heart. The reflections are recorded on a moving tape, producing a record that looks like a complex electrocardiogram. With each heartbeat, the wavy lines of the M-mode echocardiogram trace the motions of the walls and valves of the heart as it beats. The waves give doctors a line of sight through the living heart. In the past ten years, two-dimensional echocardiography has found favor in many hospitals. Instead of sending a single ray of sound through the heart, 2-D echocardiography produces a fan-shaped wedge of sound that slices through a layer of the entire heart. Two-dimensional echocardiography presents cardiologists with a moving portrait of the heart in cross section. The image can show all four chambers in action. Echocardiography enables physicians to determine the thickness of the muscle walls and the dimensions of the heart's chambers. It can reveal blood clots, tumors, heart muscle disease, defective heart valves and other problems.

Nuclear Scanning

Doctors have been injecting radioactive particles into the blood stream to study the cardiovascular system since the 1920s. But the development of the gamma, or scintillation, camera in the 1960s gave physicians a new method of studying the heart — nuclear scanning. In a nuclear scan, the gamma camera picks up traces of radioactivity emitted from isotopes injected in the blood stream. With the help of a computer, the scanner creates a color-coded map of the heart in motion. Different isotopes, developed during the 1960s and 1970s, reveal a broad range of information about the heart. By bonding to red blood cells, radioactive technetium pertechnetate enables cardiologists to study the motion of blood through the heart and the fitness of the heart wall. Injected within a day or two after a heart attack, another technetium isotope lodges in dead tissues of the heart, pinpointing damaged areas. A third radioactive marker, thallium-201, signals the presence of areas of damaged heart tissue by outlining them on the scan. Thallium follows the normal flow of blood through healthy tissues of the heart but cannot penetrate areas where the

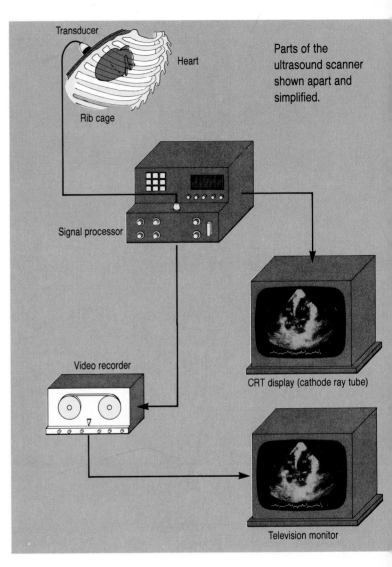

Parts of the ultrasound scanner shown apart and simplified.

In two-dimensional echocardiography, a transducer beams sound waves through the chest, records their reflections and sends electrical impulses to a signal processor. The processor creates a two-dimensional image of the beating heart displayed on a cathode ray tube terminal. By switching on a video recorder, which is wired to the signal processor, the cardiologist can produce a permanent record of the patient's echocardiogram.

Nuclear scanner camera monitors isotopes in the heart, collects information in its computer system and creates color-coded scans

R

P T P

EKG

Q S Q S

R

Amount ejected

Relative volume curve of left ventricle

Diastole

Systole

Left ventricle

Synchronized with an electrocardiogram, the nuclear scanner can measure the amount of blood ejected from the patient's left ventricle and produce a color-coded scan of the heart. The scan on the left shows the heart in diastole. The left ventricle is a round, red pool at the center. When the heart contracts, the left ventricle drives blood upward into the major arteries. Intruding on the lower right is the blood-filled spleen.

blood supply has been cut off. An area of the heart that does not show traces of thallium during a test may not be getting enough blood and oxygen. A thallium scan can locate tissue damaged by a heart attack and even detect regions that do not receive enough blood during exercise. Like the echocardiograph, the nuclear scanner is a noninvasive technique. Cardiologists can use the scanner to reach inside the heart without ever cutting the skin.

The Path to the Heart

Diagnostic developments since the 1950s have made the path to the heart less treacherous. But from the days of Ludwig Rehn to the mid-1940s, heart surgeons advanced almost blindly. Through autopsies, the defects characteristic of various congenital heart diseases were gradually pinned down, but in practice, diagnosis of heart disorders often proved impossible.

In 1923, Boston surgeons Elliott Cutler and Claude Beck and cardiologist Samuel Levine took the bold step of operating on an eleven-year-old girl suffering from mitral stenosis — a narrowing of the mitral valve between the left atrium and ventricle which causes blood to accumulate in the lungs — one of the few heart disorders that could be diagnosed fairly well. Cutler used a curved surgical knife called a valvulotome to cut a hole in one of the cusps of the mitral valve. Although the girl lived for four-and-a-half years after the operation, her condition did not markedly improve. By cutting the valve cusp, Cutler had substituted mitral incompetence for mitral stenosis. The incompetent valve allowed blood to leak back into the left atrium with every contraction of the left ventricle. This condition hampered the flow of blood out of the heart and did little to prevent the accumulation of blood in the lungs. Cutler tried the operation six more times, without success, and finally abandoned it in 1928.

While Cutler attacked mitral stenosis in the United States, another surgeon tried to correct the same problem in Great Britain. On May 6, 1925, Henry Souttar cut open the heart of a nineteen-year-old girl named Lily Hine. Souttar inserted his finger into the left atrium and gently probed the mitral valve. The cusps of the valve

118

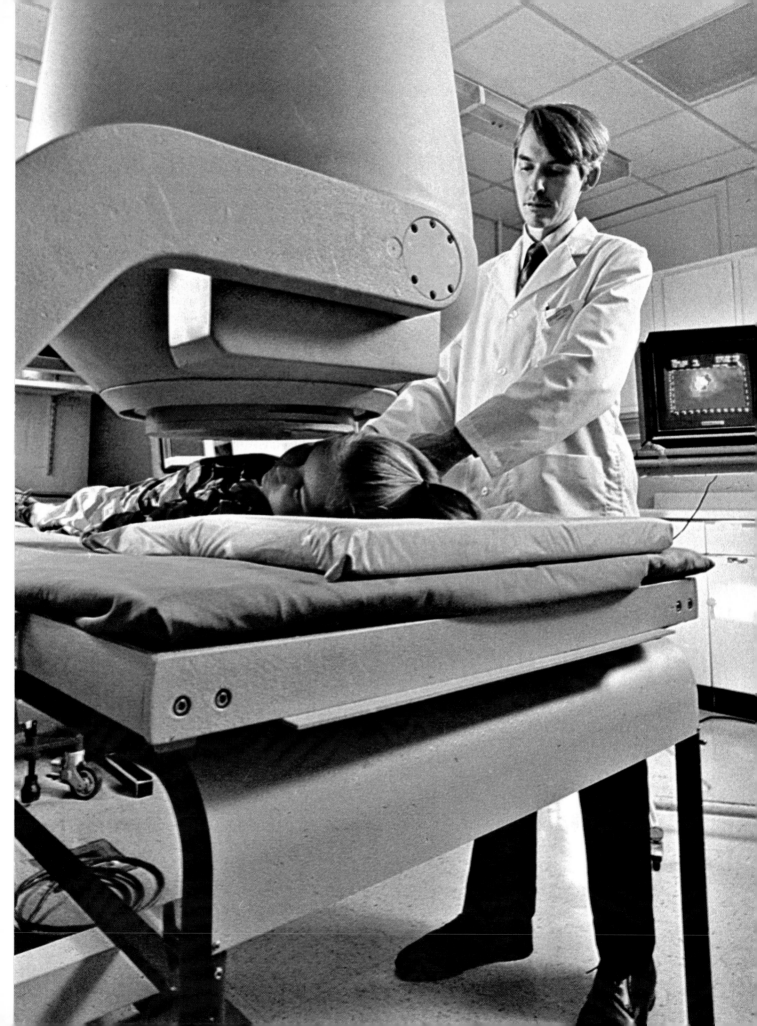

John Gibbon stands behind the heart-lung machine he used in 1953. The machine kept a patient alive for twenty-six minutes while Gibbon operated on her failing heart. The plastic case in the foreground is the machine's lung, six screens that spread blood into a film as it flows through a bath of oxygen. The large metal case is the pump itself, the heart of Gibbon's machine. His invention inaugurated the era of open-heart surgery.

pumping and oxygenating a patient's blood, thus leaving the heart dry. Gibbon had labored on the creation of his machine for twenty-two years. He had conceived the idea after sitting up all night with a patient in 1931. The woman was dying from a blood clot in her lungs. A surgeon opened her chest and removed the clot in less than seven minutes, but the woman died on the operating table. Despondent, Gibbon decided to create a machine that would save patients like the one he had just lost. For more than two decades, Gibbon and his wife experimented with different combinations of pumps, oxygenators and designs. He tested his evolving machine on cats, sometimes creeping at night through the streets of Boston to find new subjects. Gibbon's final apparatus, built with the help of IBM, consisted of one pump to draw blood from veins, a plastic case with six layers of fine mesh screen to divide the stream of blood as it trickled through a bath of oxygen, a second pump to control the flow of blood through the machine and a third to return the oxygenated blood to the patient.

In 1953, Gibbon used the heart-lung machine in an attempt to save the life of a fifteen-month-old girl. The infant's small size prohibited catheterization, however, and when Gibbon opened her chest, he did not find the atrial septal defect he expected. Soon after the operation, the child died. On May 6, 1953, Gibbon operated on an eighteen-year-old girl with an atrial septal defect, this time confirmed by catheterization. His heart-lung machine took over the responsibilities of the girl's heart and lungs for twenty-six minutes, time enough for Gibbon to open her heart and close the defect. The girl survived, but his next two patients did not. Gibbon called a halt to the use of his machine. It remained for John W. Kirklin and his associates at the Mayo Clinic in Rochester, Minnesota, to demonstrate that the heart-lung machine could be made safe and reliable for open-heart surgery. For about nine months, cross circulation in Minneapolis and the heart-lung machine in Rochester were competing methods in the only two places in the world regularly performing open-heart surgery. Machine proved superior to man. By the late 1950s, the age of the heart-lung machine had begun.

Michael DeBakey

Mending Broken Hearts

Until relatively recently, surgeons feared to enter diseased hearts and arteries. The same scalpels they used to preserve life often brought them near to hastening a death. Then, Texas surgeon Michael DeBakey took a series of bold steps that opened this forbidding territory, leaving a string of surgical innovations to mark the way.

When he entered medicine, aneurysms, deadly bulges in the walls of arteries, and occluded arteries were thought to be signs of impending death. Undaunted, DeBakey improvised surgical techniques to repair aneurysms and occlusions by replacing the diseased portion of the artery with a strong, healthy graft.

But DeBakey knew that the procedures he developed would have only limited use unless he could devise a better substitute for an ailing artery, something easier to store and more durable than arteries from cadavers. He and his assistants experimented with synthetic materials. Finally, in 1953, a machine was designed that could manufacture exactly what DeBakey wanted — a seamless, knit Dacron tube. The body, he found, adapted remarkably well to the artificial arteries. New tissue would encase the

synthetic tube, building, in effect, new arteries.

With the advent of Dacron grafts, the horizon of vascular surgery broadly and dramatically widened. DeBakey devised many uses for the invention. He replaced aortic arches and gave patients new abdominal aortas, complete with many branches. He built bypasses to reroute blood around hopelessly blocked arteries, even the delicate coronary arteries that lace the heart. And in cases where he could clear the arteries of fatty deposits, he used slips of graft material to widen the vessels. Applying this procedure to the carotid arteries eased complications in stroke patients.

Already one of the world's foremost vascular surgeons, DeBakey focused his inventive genius on the needs of the heart itself. Hearts, like pa-

tients, he knew, need rest to recover from radical surgery. Again, DeBakey found a solution. In 1966, he implanted a device in the chest of a woman whose weak heart was adjusting to its two newly implanted valves. The invention, a left ventricular bypass pump, substituted for the patient's left ventricle. After ten days, her heart was strong enough to take over and the pump was removed. This success convinced DeBakey that his dream — to build the ultimate of gadgets, an artificial heart — was possible. But he restrained his enthusiasm, knowing that much research was needed before the artificial heart could take an important place in medicine.

DeBakey demands perfection and sets an example few can match; he works tirelessly, routinely putting in twenty-hour days. His workload would fill the calendars of five surgeons. Above all, DeBakey is a compassionate man who deeply mourns the loss of a patient: "You never get over that. Never." His former patients shower him with letters of thanks. One man wrote, "The two days I was privileged to put my heart in your hands, I learned what Blake meant, 'For mercy has a human heart, pity a human face.'"

Physicians around the world quickly began experimenting with new designs. They altered the rate of blood flow through the machine, developed removable parts that could be sterilized or thrown away and invented new methods of oxygenating blood. Today, their creation is a man-made pump that for a few precious hours can assume the awesome responsibility of the heart.

Spare Parts

The idea that the organ's parts could be replaced was another development of the 1950s, leading to a new kind of heart operation — spare parts surgery. In 1952, Charles Hufnagel sewed an artificial valve into a patient's aorta. The mechanical valve helped ease the workload of her damaged aortic valve. Although Hufnagel's artificial valves, small balls inside plastic tubes, worked well enough, they tapped open and closed audibly inside his patients' chests. Some could be heard clear across a room.

Oregon surgeon Albert Starr developed artificial valves in the 1950s and successfully implanted them in patients in 1960. Starr's early valves were made of small metal or silicone balls which bobbed up and down inside a strong metal cage. A typical ball-and-cage valve replacing a mitral valve, for example, points downward into the left ventricle. During diastole, when blood drains from the atria into the ventricles, the ball drops to the furthest end of the cage, opening the valve. The contraction of the left ventricle drives the ball up into the opening of the valve, closing it and preventing blood from flowing back into the left atrium. A Teflon or Dacron skirt covers the metal ring at the base of the valve to enable surgeons to stitch the valve into the heart muscle.

Although the ball-and-cage valve developed by Starr and engineer Lowell Edwards remains the most widely used artificial heart valve in the world, it has not lacked for competitors. The surgical revolution of the 1950s and 1960s inspired the development of disc-and-cage valves, hinged valves and sutureless valves surrounded by tiny metal teeth that lodge directly in heart tissue. Some mechanical heart valves last for more than twenty years, but they also breed blood clots. Most patients with artificial heart valves must

The Starr-Edwards ball-and-cage valve is one of medicine's spare parts for the heart.

A row of sutures rim an artificial valve, about to take up residence inside the human heart.

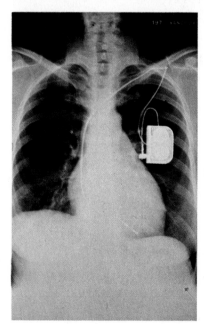

From beneath the skin, a pacemaker wires its vital spark through veins to the right ventricle.

A Coronary Bypass Operation

The coronary arteries bring blood
and life to the heart. But if the
arteries are narrowed by a build-up
of fat deposits, they can cut the
heart's blood supply to a trickle,
starving the tissues of the heart
for oxygen and bringing on the
crippling pain of angina. Blocked
coronary arteries often mean a heart
attack. Millions of Americans suffer
from serious coronary artery disease.
Those whose problems will not yield
to drug treatment are often candi-
dates for coronary bypass surgery.
An operation developed in the late
1960s, the coronary bypass has
since been performed more than
500,000 times in the U.S. alone.
Using segments of the saphenous
vein cut from the leg, where veins
are plentiful, surgeons can bypass
obstructions in coronary arteries by
stitching one end of the vein graft to
the aorta and the other to a coronary
artery past the point of obstruction,
right. Patients who are ill enough to
require surgery often receive two or
three bypasses in a single operation.
Surgeons generally use a magnifying
lens to improve their view of the
small coronary blood vessels. At
the Albany Medical Center, opposite, two surgeons peer through an
operating microscope, shown cloaked
in a sterile surgical drape. The
microscope magnifies the operating
field nine times.

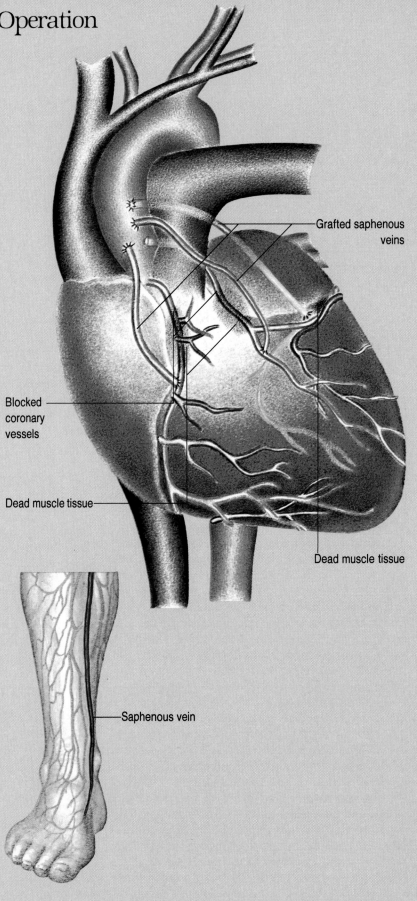

Grafted saphenous
veins

Blocked
coronary
vessels

Dead muscle tissue

Dead muscle tissue

Saphenous vein

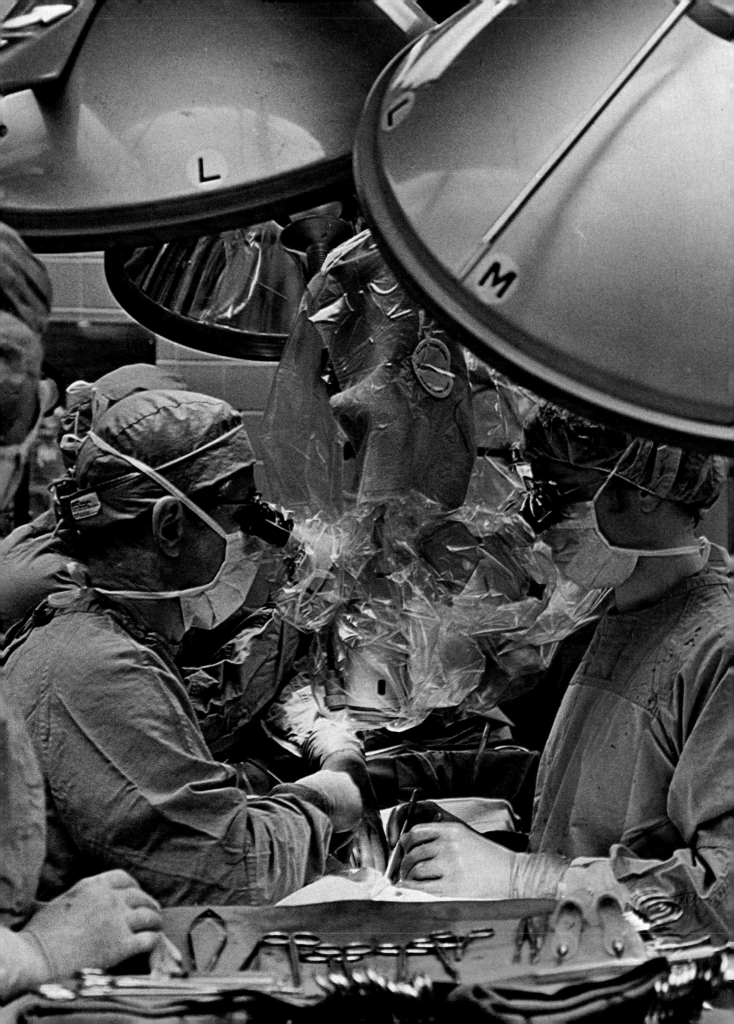

With fine-tipped forceps and a
vascular clamp, surgeons prepare a
segment of the saphenous vein taken
from the patient's leg for bypass
surgery, above. The blood-filled
syringe at the bottom of the photograph is used to flush and dilate the
vein so surgeons can check for block-
ages and other imperfections. Inside
the chest, right, surgeons grip tiny
needles with their forceps and sew a
vein graft to the heart. Watching
the delicate repair through the
operating microscope, surgeons make
a vital link, attaching one end of a
vein graft to a branch of the left
coronary artery, opposite. In a
matter of seven hours, the Albany
surgeons created five bypasses in the
patient's coronary arteries.

The purple foxglove is the source of digitalis, one of the most venerable and widely used of all cardiovascular drugs. Digitalis augments the heart's power without increasing its demand for oxygen.

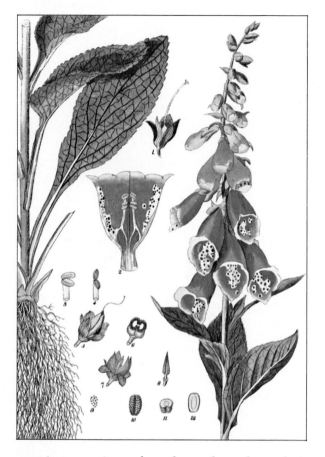

remain on anticoagulant drugs throughout their lives. To circumvent the problem of clotting and to imitate the shape of the original valve, surgeons have experimented with valves made of tissue from pigs, calves, cadavers and even from the patient. The most common criticism of tissue valves is their lack of durability, compared to artificial valves. Neither, unfortunately, is perfect.

While they were developing technologies to replace heart valves, cardiologists and surgeons also sought a device to take over the function of at least part of the heart's electrical system. In another medical miracle, they came up with one — the pacemaker.

Building on the work of physicians and electrical engineers before him, Paul Zoll, who had operated the electrocardiograph in Dwight Harken's World War II operating room, developed the first pacemaker in 1952. A patient suffering from heart block, a disorder of the heart's electrical system, went into heart failure. Zoll implanted a needle electrode in the man's chest and taped another over the ribs. When the patient's heart stopped, Zoll turned on his pacemaker and powered the man's heart electrically. Fifty-two hours later, the patient's heart resumed beating and Zoll cut off his machine.

Improvements on Zoll's pacemaker followed quickly. In 1957, C. Walton Lillehei and an electronics expert, Earl Bakken, developed a portable pacemaker. Lillehei stitched the electrodes of his device directly to the surface of the heart. Wires led out of the chest to a battery and timer strapped to the patient's abdomen. The first fully implantable pacemaker followed in 1960. In the 1960s, the original fixed-rate pacemakers, which delivered electric shocks to the heart at predetermined rates, were gradually supplanted by demand pacemakers. With a circuit to monitor heartbeat as well as one to shock the heart, the demand pacemaker delivers a current only when the rate of the heart's electrical system falls below a certain point. The electrodes of most pacemakers implanted today cling to the inside of the right ventricle, with wires leading out the right atrium to the cephalic vein in the chest. Through a small hole in the vein, the wires hook up to the battery and timer, buried beneath the skin of the chest. Batteries for pacemakers usually last anywhere from two to ten years. Today, pacemakers power the hearts of more than a million people.

The Coronary Bypass

Despite the advancements in surgical techniques, one of the most widespread heart problems, coronary artery disease, did not have a surgical solution until 1967. That year, René Favaloro, an Argentinian surgeon working in the U.S., performed the first coronary bypass operation. Surgeons had been seeking methods to improve coronary circulation since the 1930s. In 1950, Canada's Arthur Vineburg tunneled a small hole into the wall of a patient's heart, severed a nearby artery and plunged it directly into the muscle. Instead of hemorrhaging, as most doctors insisted it would, the incredible absorptive power of the heart muscle soaked up the blood. As angiograms would prove twelve years later, Vineburg's oper-

Potassium (K+), sodium (Na+) and calcium (Ca++) ions, shuttling back and forth across the cell membrane, trigger the contraction of cardiac muscle fibers. Like other cells, cardiac fibers have a biological "pump" in the cell membranes that maintains the proper balance of ions inside the cell and out. The pump is powered by energy released from a chemical reaction between adenosine triphosphate (ATP) and an enzyme, adenosine triphosphatase (ATP-ase). Digitalis inhibits the action of ATP-ase and slows the pump. Scientists believe that calcium ions then build up inside the cell and increase its contractile strength.

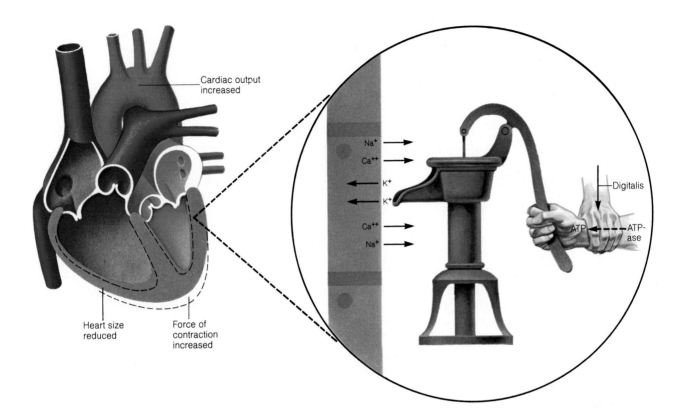

ation actually did increase the supply of blood to the heart. But it was Favaloro's bypass operation that fired the imaginations of surgeons around the world. In 1967, Favaloro cut a section of the saphenous vein from a patient's leg and used it to replace a segment of the patient's coronary artery. Later in the year, Favaloro began sewing vein grafts directly from the aorta to the severed end of a coronary artery. In early 1968, he successfully connected one end of a vein graft to the aorta and the other to the side of a blocked artery past the point of the obstruction — the model for the coronary bypass operation performed today. Favaloro's operation often provided almost miraculous relief from the crippling pain of angina pectoris and improved the flow of blood to the muscles of the heart.

It has been estimated that more than half a million coronary bypasses have been performed since 1967. But the spectacular popularity of this operation has engendered charges of abuse. One study by the Veterans Administration published in 1977 concluded that coronary bypass patients fared little better than patients on various combinations of heart medication. Later studies, however, suggested that patients undergoing coronary bypass operations might live slightly longer than similar patients kept on medication. The merits and drawbacks of coronary bypass operations are still being debated.

As important as the surgeon and his scalpel in the treatment of heart disease are the cardiologist, the pharmacologist and their small arsenal of cardiovascular drugs. For much of modern medical history, physicians had only one drug with which to combat heart disease — digitalis. British physician William Withering first publicized the effects of digitalis on the heart in 1785. Until the 1920s, doctors administered digitalis for almost all heart conditions. Nitroglycerin, still an effective drug for controlling angina pains, quinidine, an antiarrhythmic drug, and a diuretic, Salyrgan, were all introduced before World War II. Unfortunately, the biochemical workings of these drugs were poorly understood. In many cases, the effective dose and the toxic dose of a drug were very nearly the same.

Chemical Magic

The years between the end of World War II and the early 1970s saw several crucial scientific advances that dramatically improved the prospects of using drugs to control cardiovascular disease. Perhaps the most vital of these advances was the unfolding knowledge of the sympathetic nervous system, which influences the rate and power of heartbeats and regulates the dilation and constriction of the arteries and veins. Other researchers uncovered a mechanism that controls the rate at which the kidneys excrete salt and water, and thus regulates the amount of fluids in the body, including blood volume. Both of these discoveries proved invaluable to the treatment of cardiovascular disease when medical science finally became aware of the true dangers of hypertension — its links to stroke, eye damage, heart disease and kidney failure. The new-found knowledge that science could intervene in the workings of the sympathetic nervous system and the kidneys and thereby lower blood pressure touched off an explosion of pharmacological creativity that shows no signs of flagging today.

The drugs used to control hypertension fall into three categories: vasodilators, diuretics and sympatholytics. Vasodilators, such as hydralazine, lower blood pressure by relaxing muscles in peripheral arteries, decreasing resistance to the flow of blood.

Diuretics work by reducing the volume of fluids in the body, and thus the blood volume. Some also simultaneously dilate peripheral blood vessels. The most important group of diuretics is the thiazides, which include chlorothiazide and hydrochlorothiazide. Thiazides work by increasing the excretion of salt from the kidneys, which simultaneously speeds up the excretion of water. Physicians commonly use other diuretics such as spironolactone to counteract the body's loss of potassium and other side effects of the thiazides. Diuretics can also enhance the effects of other drugs used to combat high blood pressure, some of which tend to increase the amount of fluids that the body retains.

The sympatholytics interfere with the functioning of the sympathetic nervous system. Some, like clonidine and methyldopa, work mainly on the brain and spinal cord and are often called central nervous system blockers. Others affect principally the peripheral nervous system or the ends of nerve fibers in the blood vessels themselves. Described as peripheral nervous system blockers, these drugs include guanethidine, prazosin, phentolamine and others. Another drug, propranolol, seems to affect both the central and peripheral nervous systems. One of a family of drugs called beta blockers, propranolol can help lower blood pressure, eliminate angina pains and control cardiac arrhythmias. Since hypertension is usually incurable, these drugs are indispensable for protecting the brain, heart and kidneys from the ravages of high blood pressure.

Drugs to control hypertension are only a small part of the cardiologist's battery of drugs. An anticoagulant called heparin keeps blood flowing smoothly through the tubes, pumps and chambers of the heart-lung machine. The blood clots that commonly form on artificial valves could be nearly as deadly as heart valve disease without oral anticoagulants such as warfarin. To control cardiac arrhythmias that will not yield to surgery, cardiologists often administer drugs such as procainamide and disopyramide.

One of the most promising families of drugs on the horizon today is the calcium blockers. Already used in Europe and Japan, calcium blockers — verapamil, nifedipine and others — influence the heart's electrical system by inhibiting the flow of calcium ions across cell membranes. Calcium blockers can help reduce angina pains from coronary artery spasms and help calm cardiac arrhythmias. Some scientists even speculate that calcium blockers may eventually help prevent second heart attacks and reduce the need for coronary bypass operations.

The enthusiasm that surrounds the impending arrival of calcium blockers in the United States illustrates how far the chemical treatment of cardiovascular disease has come in the past fifty years. In 1930, doctors usually administered digitalis or nothing. Today, cardiologists have a pharmacopoeia at their disposal, chemical magic every bit as remarkable as the wizardry of the heart surgeon.

Court of Last Resort

December 3, 1967, may prove to be the most controversial day in twentieth-century medical history. On that day, a South African heart surgeon, Christiaan Barnard, cut out a man's heart and gave him another. Barnard's heart transplant epitomizes the great hope and the great despair of man's attempts to restore the human heart. Barnard managed to keep his first patient, Louis Washkansky, alive for eighteen days, and his second, Philip Blaiberg, for almost six hundred. He gave his patients new hearts, but he could not make their bodies accept the gift. To protect itself from infection, the body's immune system regards all alien tissue as the enemy and makes no distinction between deadly bacteria and a lifesaving heart. The euphoria of the medical world quickly gave way to disillusionment as transplant recipients faltered and died, their bodies rejecting the hearts that kept them alive. The number of transplants fell from 101 in 1968 to 47 in 1969, and only 17 in 1970.

A heart transplant is not the most technically difficult operation. Techniques vary, but the general procedure leaves part of the patient's atria intact, along with the major veins bringing blood back to the left and right sides of the heart. The donor's heart is then stitched onto the remaining sections of the patient's atria and connected to the pulmonary artery and aorta.

Although Christiaan Barnard performed the first heart transplant, much of the credit for making the operation possible must go to surgeon Norman Shumway of Stanford University. In 1958 at Stanford, Shumway and surgeon Richard Lower began a series of experiments on dogs to find exactly where to cut the damaged heart, how to protect vital nerves, which drugs to use and how to preserve the donor heart before transplant. It was Shumway's techniques that

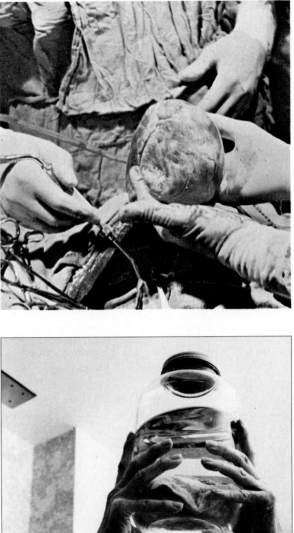

Barnard and other surgeons adopted in 1968. The great majority of transplants in the U.S. since 1970 are Shumway's, and his success in keeping transplant recipients alive far outstrips that of any other surgeon in the world. At Stanford, the percentage of patients surviving for one year after a heart transplant rose from 22 percent in 1968 to 69 percent in 1978. About half of Shumway's patients survive for more than five years. The transplant operations performed by Shumway increase both the length and the quality of the patients' lives.

Shumway's surgical skill is not the only reason for his success. The California surgeon's patients survive because they are carefully selected as being likely to survive the operation and the difficult years of treatment that follow. After the transplant, the real work of keeping the patient alive begins. For a long period after the operation, the patient must undergo weekly biopsies of heart tissue (small pieces snipped from inside the heart by a pair of forceps inserted through the jugular vein) and for the rest of his life he must take drugs to prevent rejection. New drugs like antithymocyte globulin and cyclosporin A prevent the body's immune system from destroying the donor heart. But as Shumway has said, "Transplantation is a court of last resort when the alternative is death."

Heart transplants remain a kind of surgical and pharmacological sleight of hand, an inestimable blessing for men and women with dying hearts. Through medical cajoling and coaxing, Norman Shumway, Richard Lower and a few other doctors around the world can sometimes trick the body into tolerating a substitute heart.

A New Wave of Progress

The medical miracles of the last thirty years may be outdone by those to come. The echocardiograph, the pacemaker and the heart transplant may be overshadowed by a new wave of medical progress, a daring technical surge forward that may soon replace the heart altogether.

Scientists at the Mayo Clinic in Rochester, Minnesota, have been working for the past ten years on a new device that may make echocardiography and angiocardiography seem almost

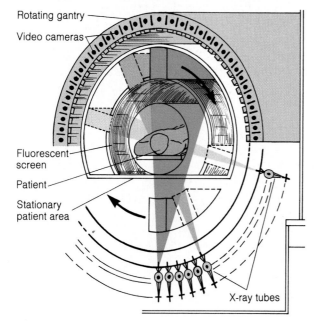

Rotating gantry

Video cameras

Fluorescent screen

Patient

Stationary patient area

X-ray tubes

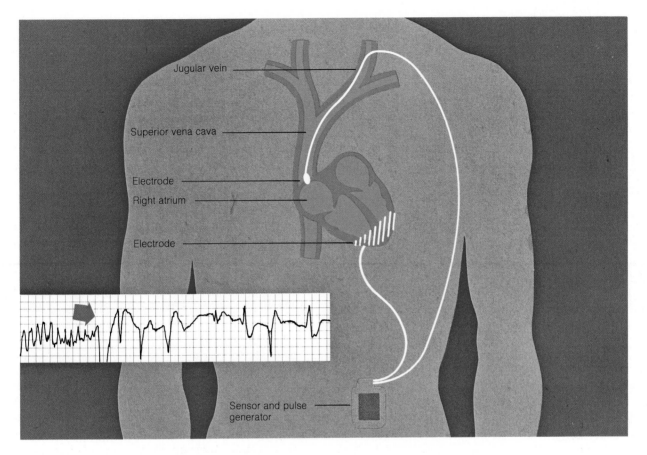

Jugular vein

Superior vena cava

Electrode

Right atrium

Electrode

Sensor and pulse generator

primitive. Under the leadership of physiologist Earl Wood, doctors, engineers and computer specialists have created a revolutionary new device for peering inside the human body, the Dynamic Spatial Reconstructor (DSR).

The DSR takes the same principles that underlie computerized axial tomography (CAT), a diagnostic tool that recently won its creators a Nobel Prize, and moves a step further. Like the CAT scanner, the DSR beams X-rays through the body and converts them into images on a television screen. Instead of producing horizontal slices of the portion of the body being X-rayed, the DSR gives a full-sized three-dimensional image of the organ in motion, the beating heart or the expanding lungs.

The X-ray system of the DSR, a seventeen-ton, turbine-shaped chamber called the gantry, contains fourteen X-ray tubes in a semicircular array. (Future versions will contain twenty-

From an orderly rhythm of life, the beat of an ailing heart can degenerate into a chaotic, malignant squirming called fibrillation. Ventricular fibrillation often means death, especially when its victims are beyond the reach of doctors or paramedics. But a new device developed by Michel Mirowski and other doctors, the automatic implantable defibrillator, holds out hope for some people with unpredictable hearts. Implanted beneath the skin, Mirowski's defibrillator consists of a pulse generator and a sensor wired to two electrodes. The device monitors the heart, detects dangerous rhythms and delivers up to four 700-volt shocks to jolt a patient back to life.

eight.) A crescent-shaped fluorescent screen forms the other half of the circle, directly across from the X-ray guns. The patient lies inside the turbine, at the center of the circle, and the whole gantry revolves once every four seconds while the X-ray guns fire off sixty beams a second. The X-ray images produced on the fluorescent screen are recorded by television cameras and stored on video discs. A computer transforms the information on the discs into a series of numbers, and a second computer changes the numbers into three-dimensional images that are displayed on the television screen.

The speed at which the DSR takes X-rays enables it to produce slow-motion or stop-action images of living organs. Doctors can see blood moving through the heart or air through the lungs. A DSR image of the heart can be cut open or dissolved, bit by bit, until only the coronary artery tree remains. The DSR can then select and display the tiniest segments of the arteries to help doctors locate the most minute damage, perhaps before a problem becomes serious.

Doctors at the Mayo Clinic recently used the DSR to scan their first human patient. A complete DSR scan exposes the patient to about as much radiation as two chest X-rays. And its potential diagnostic uses are virtually limitless. It can observe a beating heart in a patient's chest, and bring what it sees, in minute detail, to the physicians charged with protecting that heart.

The DSR locates heart problems, but it cannot cure them. Another new medical technology, the automatic implantable defibrillator, may soon help protect patients from one of the most dangerous of all heart afflictions, the electrical malfunction known as ventricular fibrillation.

Developed by Michel Mirowski and a team of scientists at Sinai Hospital in Baltimore, the implantable defibrillator serves the same purpose as the powerful external defibrillators that line the walls of hospital operating rooms and intensive care units. When a patient's heart rhythm degenerates into the deadly, chaotic rippling called fibrillation, doctors can apply the electrodes of a defibrillator to the patient's chest and literally shock him back to life. Mirowski's invention takes the defibrillator several steps further. Im-

planted in the patient, the device continually monitors the heart and delivers a lifesaving shock if it detects irregular rhythms.

Mirowski's implantable defibrillator consists of two electrodes inside the chest and a pulse generator and sensor implanted under the skin. One electrode hangs inside the superior vena cava; the second is sewn to the apex of the heart. Through the electrodes, the sensor monitors the beating heart. If the sensor detects fibrillation, it signals the pulse generator to shock the heart after a fifteen-second delay. If the first shock does not start the fibrillating heart, the device can deliver three more shocks at fifteen-second intervals. At least twenty-four of Mirowski's patients already carry the implantable defibrillator inside their chests. Their failing hearts have responded to its electrical promptings nearly fifty times. Once it is fully tested, Mirowski's device may protect the spark of life in hundreds of thousands of patients with untrustworthy hearts.

Perhaps the most remarkable testimony to the progress of heart medicine is the development of the artificial heart. For over a decade, surgeons have been using a variety of unlikely looking temporary pumps, such as the left ventricular assist device (LVAD), in desperate attempts to save patients near death on the operating table. Only a few of those patients, a very few, have survived. At the Texas Heart Institute in Houston, surgeon Denton Cooley has twice implanted artificial hearts in dying patients. Both operations were temporary measures to keep patients alive until a heart suitable for transplantation could be found. But no surgeon has yet attempted to replace the human heart with a permanent manmade pump. A permanent artificial heart, a device that stands a good chance of keeping a patient alive for weeks, months or even years, is today the dream of physicians and heart patients around the world.

In the United States, the driving force behind the development of the artificial heart is Willem Kolff, a seventy-year-old bioengineer and surgeon who invented the artificial kidney. In 1957, at the Cleveland Clinic, Kolff began implanting artificial hearts in dogs. One of his early efforts kept a dog alive for ninety minutes. Since 1967,

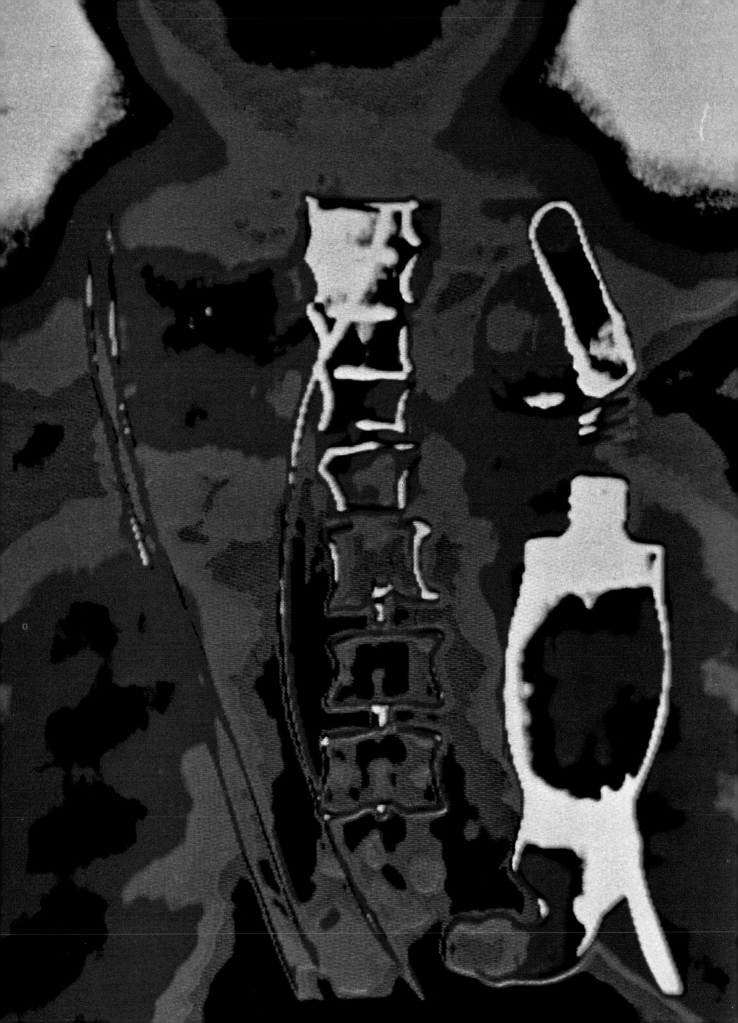

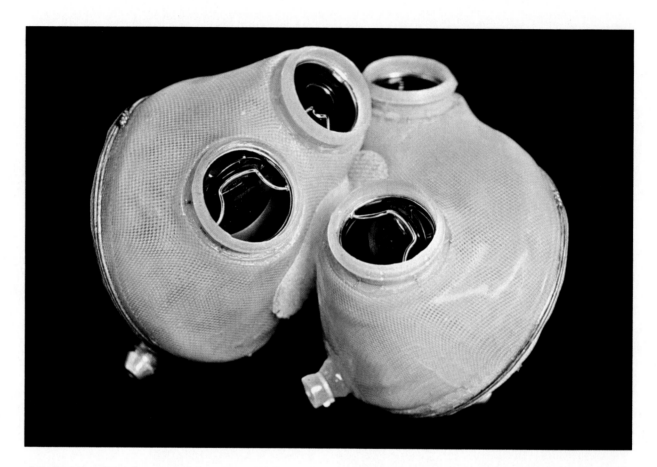

An aluminum base, four mechanical valves, and two flexible polyurethane ventricles form the Jarvik-7 artificial heart. Powered by an air compressor outside the body, the Jarvik-7 may soon pump blood inside a human chest.

at the University of Utah in Salt Lake City, Kolff has worked steadily on a succession of artificial hearts of various design, some powered by batteries, some by plutonium.

But the difficulty of safely putting a small power plant inside the human chest finally forced Kolff and his colleagues to take a new approach. The first artificial heart permanently installed in a human being may well throb to the beat of pulses of compressed air.

In 1970, Kolff added to his staff a young medical student named Robert Jarvik, a former carpenter and jeweler with a formal education in biomechanics. The new team member quickly designed a smaller, more efficient artificial heart. Since April, 1978, his latest model, the Jarvik-7, has been pumping water in a laboratory tank. Another Jarvik-7 kept a calf named Tennyson alive for 268 days, and a third sustained the bodily functions of a woman for two hours after she

had been declared legally dead. The U.S. Food and Drug Administration recently granted the University of Utah team permission to implant the Jarvik-7 in a human patient if it might save a life that would otherwise be lost.

The Jarvik-7 consists of four artificial valves, two polyurethane ventricles on aluminum bases and two small tubes leading from the bottom of the ventricles through the chest wall and outside the body. In an actual operation, the chief thoracic surgeon at the University of Utah, William DeVries, would cut away the useless ventricles of the patient's heart and sew Dacron cuffs on the atria, the pulmonary artery and the aorta. The ventricles of the Jarvik-7 snap on to the cuffs — like Tupperware, says DeVries. Once the artificial heart were started, pulses of compressed air would push on diaphragms inside the ventricles and pump blood out of the heart. With the pulses stopped, blood would fill the ventricles.

More than one hundred hearts, mostly from calves and sheep, line the walls of a laboratory at the Cleveland Clinic, where scientists have been testing artificial hearts in animals for twenty-five years.

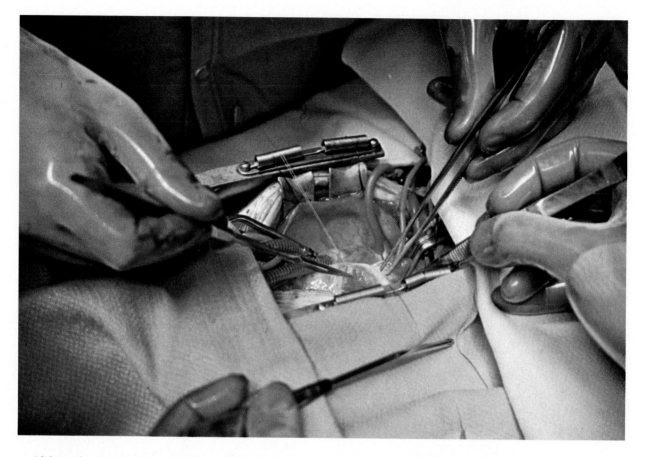

Although the Jarvik-7 might someday offer a desperately ill patient new life, it would be a restricted life, always dependent on a compressor and a few emergency cylinders of air. The flesh surrounding the flexible tubes which lead from the compressor to the Jarvik-7 would be fertile ground for infection, a problem that has plagued tests with laboratory animals. Any patient hooked up to the present version of the Jarvik-7 would have to spend his life in a one-floor home or apartment near the University of Utah, submit to daily monitoring by doctors and probably never leave Salt Lake City.

The psychological price of the artificial heart could make its monetary price, which is currently about $25,000, seem small by comparison. But any candidate for the operation would have been so near death for so long that the artificial heart, with all its liabilities, might seem a blessing. As many as 50,000 people each year could theoreti-

cally be granted a longer life through the use of an implantable artificial heart.

The work of Kolff, Jarvik and their colleagues is one of the new frontiers of heart care, the strange land where biological life and mechanical life overlap. And perhaps no other single technique or innovation better illustrates the prodigious strides that man's knowledge of the heart has taken in the last thirty years. Physicians have learned that the heart can be cut open, sutured, stopped, restarted, chilled and bypassed. Recognized early, heart diseases that once meant a brief, weary life can now be cured, the damaged heart made whole. Kolff and his colleagues believe they can replace the heart. But even the creators of the artificial heart readily acknowledge that their proud pump is no substitute for the real thing. Even in the age of biomedical miracles, the heart remains one of the most durable and fascinating miracles of all.

*Kristina displays two hallmarks of
a successful open-heart operation,
a scar and a smile. Surgeons at
Children's Hospital in Boston put
two Dacron patches and new life
into her small heart.*

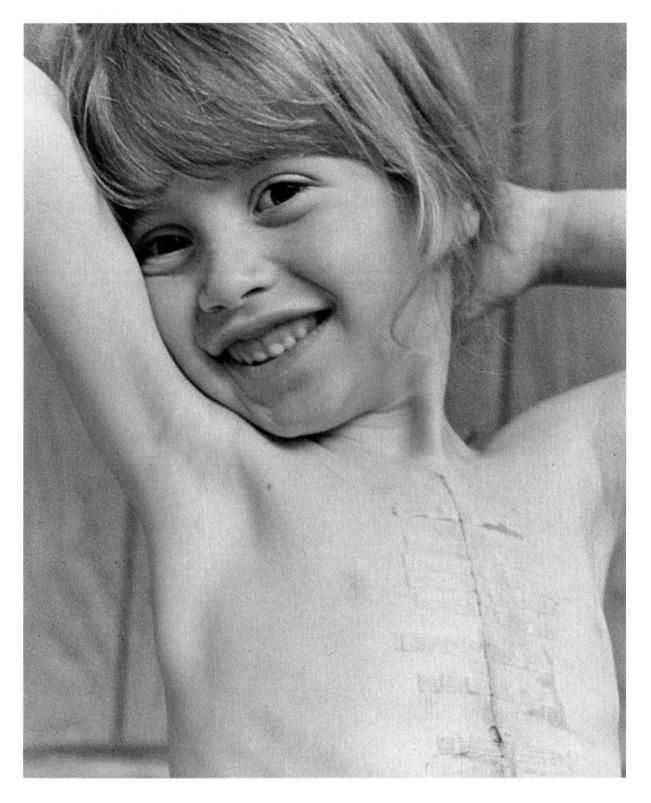

141

Appendix 1: How to Recognize a Heart Attack

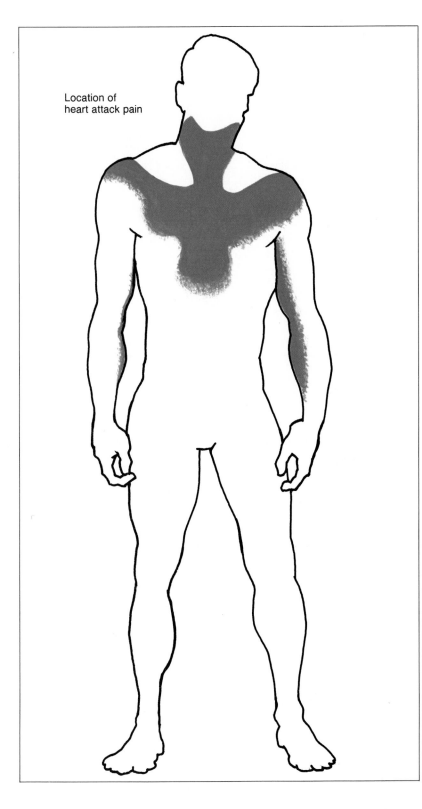

Location of heart attack pain

Most chest pains signify nothing more than muscle strain, arthritis or indigestion. But sometimes a chest pain warns of an impending heart attack. Since even a few minutes' delay in getting medical attention can be deadly, prompt recognition of the signs and symptoms of a heart attack can make a lifesaving difference.

Symptoms: If you experience any of the following sensations, seek help at once:

1. Prolonged squeezing or pressure in the center of the chest, either severe or relatively mild. Discomfort may spread to one or both arms, shoulder, upper abdomen, jaw or back.
2. Nausea, cold sweating, dizziness, shortness of breath or difficulty in breathing.
3. A feeling of extreme weakness or dread.

Signs: If you observe the following signs in another person, suspect a heart attack:

1. Unconsciousness
2. Moist, cool, bluish skin
3. Absent pulse
4. Lack of breathing
5. Dilated pupils

Emergency steps: If the person's condition does not appear to be grave, and there is a hospital nearby, drive him to the emergency room.

If the person's life appears to be in immediate danger, call for an ambulance. If you are familiar with resuscitation techniques, and breathing and pulse are absent, begin CPR. (see next page).

The Basic Steps of CPR

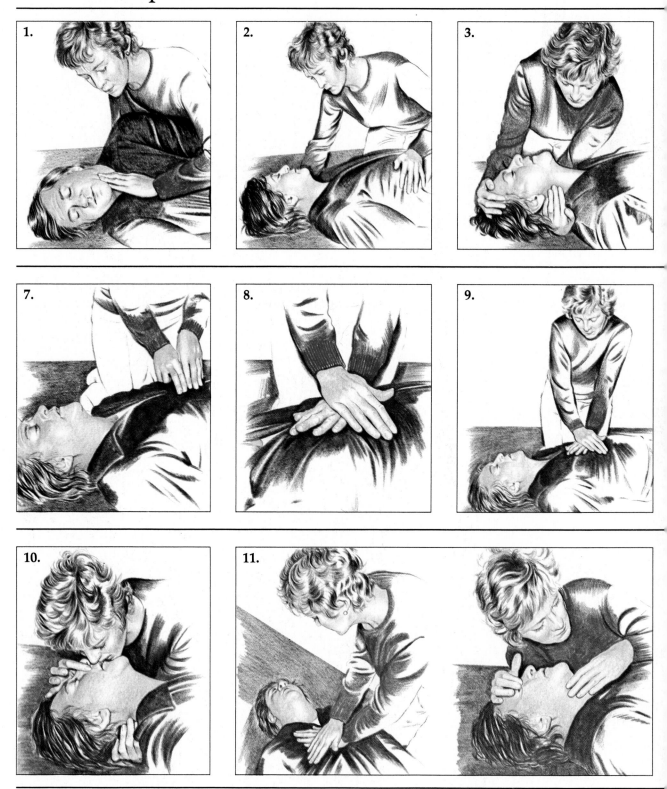

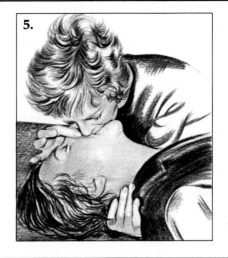
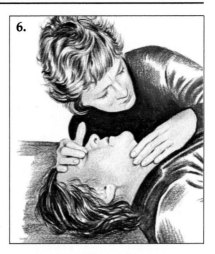

Two thirds of all heart attack deaths occur before the victim reaches a hospital. Many of these lives might have been saved if a trained bystander had been there to give CPR — cardiopulmonary resuscitation. Millions of Americans have been trained in CPR, and thousands of lives have been saved. Courses in CPR are available in many communities. Outlined here are the basic steps:

1. Check for signs of cardiac arrest: unconsciousness and lack of pulse. Call for medical help.

2. If you suspect cardiac arrest, place the victim in position for CPR by rolling him onto his back.

3. Open the airway by extending and lifting the neck. Tilt chin upward.

4. Check for signs of breathing: feel and listen for air movement at mouth and nose; look for movement in chest. Clear foreign objects from the mouth.

5. If the victim is not breathing, begin rescue breathing immediately: Pinching the victim's nose, breathe rapidly into his mouth four times. Watch for chest rise and feel for pulse.

6. If chest rises and pulse is present, continue rescue breathing. If chest does not rise and pulse is absent, begin chest compressions.

7. Kneel beside the victim. Find the lower tip of the breastbone. Two finger-breadths above this point, place the heel of one hand, with the other hand on top.

8. With your body directly above the victim's, thrust forcefully and rhythmically fifteen times, at the rate of one thrust per second. Thrust hard enough to depress the breastbone an inch-and-a-half.

9. Between each downstroke, release, lifting hands upward while still keeping the heel of the hand in contact with the chest.

10. Lean over quickly, open the airway and take a deep breath. Pinch the victim's nose, then quickly breathe in twice into his mouth.

11. Repeat this cycle (fifteen chest compressions followed by two breaths) until medical help arrives or the victim regains pulse.

Appendix 2: Recovery from a Heart Attack

Eighty percent of all heart attack survivors make a full recovery. In the coronary care unit, hospital staff monitor the patient continuously during the critical stage. While still in the hospital, the patient begins a program of slowly increasing physical activity. Rehabilitation continues at home with moderate exercise.

Exercise plays a dual role for the cardiac patient by restoring confidence and strengthening the heart. A treadmill test defines a patient's safe exertion level and dictates the pace of an exercise regimen. Since sudden or strenuous movement can injure a healing heart, a coronary fitness program guides the patient through slow, gradual stages. They range from short, leisurely walks to swimming, bicycling, even jogging, depending upon the individual's condition.

Although eventually recovering much of its strength, the heart remains vulnerable immediately after a heart attack. The patient can speed his recovery by following basic guidelines. Drugs can relieve pain and prevent clotting. Elimination of cigarettes, fatty foods and excess stress could help ward off a second attack.

A Guide to Selected Foods

All food portions are 100 grams	Saturated fatty acids (gr)	Polyunsaturated fatty acids (gr)	Cholesterol (mg)	Sodium (mg)
DAIRY FOODS:				
Swiss cheese	17.8	1.0	92	264
cottage cheese, creamed	2.9	0.1	15	404
cottage cheese, uncreamed	0.3	trace	7	12
American cheese, pasteurized process	19.7	1.0	94	1450
whole milk, 3.3% fat	2.1	0.1	14	50
low fat milk, partially skimmed, 1% fat	0.7	trace	4	50
dry whole milk	16.7	0.7	97	536
yogurt, low-fat, plain	1.0	trace	6	70
ice cream, vanilla	6.7	0.4	45	80
EGGS:				
whole, raw (fresh or frozen)	3.4	1.5	548	118
yolk only, fresh, raw	9.9	4.3	1602	52
white only	0	0	0	151
FISH:				
shrimp, boiled	0.2	0.5	150	161
salmon, red, canned, liquid and solids	1.8	0.5	35	387
tuna, canned in water, light	0.2	0.7	63	339
Alaska king crab	0.2	0.6	100	NA*
VEGETABLES:				
brussels sprouts	0.6	0.2	0	14
spinach	trace	0.1	0	71
asparagus	trace	0.1	0	2
onion	0.2	1.0	0	2
potato, white, peeled, boiled	trace	0.1	0	2
mushrooms (American)	trace	0.1	0	15
carrots	0.1	0.1	0	47
FRUITS:				
avocado, California	2.0	2.0	0	10
apple, whole	trace	trace	0	1
strawberry	trace	0.1	0	1
orange	trace	trace	0	1
banana	0.1	0.1	0	1
POULTRY:				
chicken, broiler-fryer, cooked or roasted, dark meat	2.7	2.3	93	NA
chicken, broiler-fryer, cooked or roasted, light meat	1.3	1.0	85	NA
turkey, light meat, cooked or roasted, no skin	1.0	0.9	69	NA
turkey, dark meat, cooked or roasted, no skin	2.4	2.2	85	NA
MEATS:				
T-bone steak, broiled, 56% lean, 44% fat	18.0	1.6	95	65
sirloin steak, broiled, 66% lean, 34% fat	13.3	1.2	95	65
hamburger (ground beef) regular grind, broiled	9.5	1.0	95	65
heart, braised, lean	1.8	1.1	274	104
liver, beef, fried	2.9	1.5	438	118
bacon, fried and drained	18.1	5.4	85	1957
ham, cooked or roasted	3.0	1.0	55	1310
pork loin	9.8	3.1	90	65
sausage, pork, cooked	11.7	4.0	83	958
leg of lamb, cooked, separable lean	4.0	0.6	100	68
veal, leg, broiled, 79% lean, 21% fat	4.7	0.7	101	81
GRAIN, CEREAL PRODUCTS:				
rice, white, boiled	0.05	0.12	NA	3
shredded wheat	0.04	1.33	NA	1
spaghetti, cooked	trace	trace	NA	1
wheat germ, cooked	trace	trace	NA	4

*NA — data not available

Source: USDA

Appendix 3: Diet

Fatty Acid Content of Fats and Oils

Item (100 grams)	Saturated fatty acids (grams)	Polyunsaturated fatty acids (grams)
butter	50.5	3.0
lard (pork)	39.2	11.2
coconut oil	86.5	1.8
corn oil	12.7	58.7
safflower oil	9.1	74.5
margarine		
hydrogenated soybean		
oil, stick	14.9	14.4
corn oil, tub	14.2	31.9
safflower oil, tub	13.4	48.4
French salad dressing (commercial)	9.5	21.7
Italian salad dressing (commercial)	7.0	28.0
mayonnaise (safflower and soybean)	8.6	55.0
shortening (household — lard and vegetable oil)	40.3	10.9

Source: USDA

The role of nutrition in heart disease has not been proven conclusively, but evidence from decades of study implicates foods rich in cholesterol, saturated fats and simple sugars. The typical American diet, laden with fatty meats, rich desserts and snack foods, may lie at the root of our national vulnerability for coronary heart disease. In less developed countries where the fare is leaner, heart disease is rare.

The chart on the opposite page shows the cholesterol, sodium and fatty acids content of selected food items from each food group. Foods high in cholesterol and saturated fats should be eaten sparingly by heart patients and other people with a high risk of coronary heart disease. The American Heart Association recommends restricting cholesterol intake to 300 milligrams a day (roughly the amount in one large egg yolk). Many heart patients and hypertensives must also limit their intake of sodium (salt), which is especially abundant in cheeses, snack foods, luncheon meats and seasonings.

The chart above left compares the fatty acids content of various types of fats and oils. Most vegetable oils are high in polyunsaturates while saturated fatty acids are found primarily in animal products. A diet that is high in saturated fats tends to increase the level of cholesterol in the blood stream. Polyunsaturates supply essential fatty acids and may help regulate cholesterol levels.

149

The Effects of Exercise on Cardiovascular Fitness

Levels of Conditioning	Activity	Cardiovascular Benefits
1	Walking 1 – 2 mph	Not strenuous enough to promote cardiovascular fitness.
	Light housework	Too sporadic and mild to provide adequate dynamic exercise
2	Golf, using cart	Improves arm strength, but not rigorous enough to build cardiovascular endurance
	Bowling	Not continuous enough for effective conditioning
	Walking 3 mph	Sufficient for someone with a low exercise capacity
3	Mopping, vacuuming, cleaning windows	Good endurance training if continuous for 20 – 30 minutes
	Walking 3.5 mph	Good conditioning exercise
	Bicycling 8 mph	Promotes cardiovascular strength
4	Volleyball, badminton	Good endurance activity when played rigorously
	Walking 4 – 5 mph	Excellent cardiovascular conditioning activity
	Water skiing	Dangerous for person with known or hidden heart disease
5	Ice or roller skating	Excellent when performed continuously
	Bicycling 12 mph	Builds endurance, trains cardiovascular system
	Jogging 5 mph	Excellent conditioner
	Downhill skiing	Not continuous enough to build endurance
6	Cross-country skiing	Superb dynamic exercise
	Running 6 or more mph	Promotes cardiovascular strength
	Squash, handball	Dangerous to someone out of condition. Can build endurance in skilled player when continuous for 30 minutes or more

Warnings and What to do About Them

Symptom	Probable Cause	What to Do
Fluttering pulse	Extra heartbeats or cardiac arrhythmia	
Rapid heartbeat	Extra heartbeats or cardiac arrhythmia	
Chest pain	Possible hidden heart disease	
Elevated heart rate even 5 – 10 minutes after end of exercise	Exercise too vigorous. Increase exercise more slowly.	
Prolonged breathlessness 10 minutes or more after completing exercise	Exercise too taxing. Reduce activity level to lower portion of target zone.	
Muscle ache or charley horse	Poor muscle tone from lack of conditioning. Apply moist heat, reduce exercise level.	

In search of strength, muscle tone or tranquility, millions of Americans have become avid exercise enthusiasts. But exercise does more than improve the physique or tame an irritable temperament. Its most important benefit is far more basic: The right kind of exercise, when practiced regularly, can provide protection against heart attack.

Swimming, walking, skating and running are aerobic exercises; they all involve the continuous movement of large groups of muscles. Aerobic exercise performed at the correct rate promotes cardiovascular fitness, an optimal state of health in which the heart pumps more strongly, slowly and with greater efficiency. Static activities such as waterskiing and weightlifting do not improve circulatory health, although they can boost muscle strength and size.

The chart on the opposite page compares the cardiovascular benefits of various types of exercise.

At top left are common warning signs that can result from exercise, and what to do about them.

The chart, bottom left, illustrates the correct exercise level for achieving cardiovascular fitness. The top line shows the maximum heart rate attainable for each age group. The target zone is 70 to 85% of the maximum rate. Twenty to thirty minutes of aerobic exercise three times a week can produce a maximum fitness level in three to six months.

Chart: Heart rate in beats per minute vs. Age in years, showing "Maximal attainable heart rate", "85% level", "70% level", and the TARGET ZONE.

Maximal attainable heart rate values: 200, 194, 188, 182, 176, 171, 165, 159

85% level values: 170, 165, 160, 155, 150, 145, 140, 135, 130

70% level values: 140, 136, 132, 128, 124, 119, 115, 111, 107

Glossary

actin a muscle protein. Overlapping filaments of actin and another protein, myosin, inside muscle cells enable muscles to contract.

alveolus a tiny air sac in the lungs where blood exchanges carbon dioxide for oxygen.

anastomosis a link between two blood vessels or organs.

anesthetic a substance that causes loss of sensation, especially to pain.

aneurysm abnormal swelling that forms on a blood vessel or heart wall. Aneurysms are due to weakening of the wall by disease or injury.

angina pectoris pain or tightness in the chest caused by an insufficient supply of blood to the heart.

angiocardiography a diagnostic technique that uses opaque contrast dyes injected into the blood stream to outline blood vessels, the heart and other organs of the body on X-ray photographs.

anterior descending artery a branch of the left coronary artery that brings blood down the front of the heart to both ventricles.

anticoagulants drugs that interfere with the clotting of blood. They are used during surgery and as long-term therapy for patients with artificial heart valves.

antiseptic a substance that destroys or inhibits the growth of microorganisms that cause disease.

aortic valve the valve at the junction of the left ventricle and the aorta; one of the heart's two semilunar valves.

arrhythmia an irregular heart rhythm.

arteries blood vessels that carry blood away from the heart.

arterioles small arteries.

arteriosclerosis a condition known as hardening of the arteries in which the artery walls become thick and rigid.

atherosclerosis a form of arteriosclerosis in which the inner lining of an artery becomes thick and hard due to build-up of fatty substances. These deposits narrow the diameter of the artery and reduce the flow of blood to the heart. Atherosclerosis is the cause of most heart attacks.

atrial septal defect a hole in the septum between the atria.

atrioventricular canal in the embryo, the canal that joins the primitive atrium to the ventricles. It divides into two separate channels, the sites of the atrioventricular valves, during normal fetal development.

atrioventricular (AV) node a cluster of cells located between the atria and ventricles, which relays electrical signals to the bundle of His.

atrioventricular valves the tricuspid valve and the mitral valve, which connect the atria to the ventricles.

atrium one of two upper chambers of the heart. The right atrium receives blood returning to the heart from the body. The left atrium receives oxygen-filled blood from the lungs.

automatic implantable defibrillator a device implanted in the body that detects irregular heart rhythms and delivers an electric shock to the heart to correct the rhythm.

automaticity the ability of certain cells, especially cardiac muscle cells, to generate an electrical impulse spontaneously.

baroreceptors nerve endings located in blood vessel walls which become stimulated by changes in pressure.

bundle of His a mass of fibers running from the atrioventricular node to the ventricles. It relays impulses from the AV node to the heart muscle.

bypass surgery surgery that uses a natural or synthetic blood vessel to bypass blockage in another blood vessel.

calcium blockers a new family of drugs that affects the flow of calcium ions across the cell membranes of cardiac muscle cells. Calcium blockers may help combat angina pectoris and arrhythmias.

capillaries the smallest blood vessels; they carry oxygen-filled blood to all parts of the body.

cardiac output the amount of blood the heart can pump each minute, determined by the frequency of stroke and the volume of blood.

cardiac veins veins that bring deoxygenated blood from the muscles of the heart to the right atrium.

cardiology the scientific study of the heart, its functions and diseases.

cardiomyopathy disease of the heart muscle. It usually takes one of two forms. In the hypertrophic variety, the heart muscle thickens, sometimes leading to heart murmur and rhythm disturbances. Congestive cardiomyopathy is the enlargement of the heart cavity. Blood clots are a danger in this disease.

cardiovascular system the heart and blood vessels. Arteries transport blood to the tissues; veins return the blood to the heart.

carotid artery a major artery carrying blood to the brain.

catheter a thin tube that can be inserted into blood vessels, the heart or other organs. Cardiac catheterization is the diagnostic technique of inserting a catheter through veins or arteries into the heart.

cholesterol fatlike substance present in the blood and other body tissues and in meats and dairy foods. High blood concentrations of cholesterol are often associated with coronary heart disease.

chordae tendineae inelastic tendons that reach from the tops of papillary muscles in the ventricles to the cusps of the mitral and tricuspid valves.

circumflex artery a branch of the left coronary artery that brings blood to the left atrium and ventricle.

circus movement phenomenon in which the heart's electrical impulses continue firing instead of dying out after running their course. Heart flutter and fibrillation can result.

coarctation of the aorta a heart defect that constricts the aorta near the point where it branches to bring blood to the upper and lower body.

collateral vessels small blood vessels that reroute blood from a nearby main artery which has become blocked.

congenital heart defect any of a number of abnormalities of the heart present at birth.

coronary angiography the diagnostic technique of using contrast dyes injected into the blood stream and X-rays to make the coronary arteries visible. Also known as coronary arteriography.

coronary arteries arteries ascending from the aorta and curving down over the top of the heart. They transport blood to the heart muscle.

coronary heart disease any heart disorder caused by decreased blood supply to the heart; most often caused by atherosclerosis.

coronary sinus a blood vessel that carries blood from cardiac veins into the right atrium.

cross circulation a technique for linking the circulation of a patient with that of a donor to let blood bypass the patient's heart during surgery.

defibrillator a device which sends electrical current into the heart in order to stop fibrillation, a deadly rhythm disturbance, and allow the heart to resume a normal rhythm.

152

diabetes mellitus a chronic disorder marked by the inability to metabolize carbohydrates; usually due to a lack of insulin, a hormone that burns blood sugar.

diastole the relaxation stage of each heartbeat between contractions, when the heart muscle fills with blood.

digitalis a drug that increases the contractile power of heart muscle; extracted from the foxglove plant.

diuretics drugs such as the thiazides that increase the body's excretion of salt and water; used in the treatment of high blood pressure.

ductus arteriosus a short blood vessel connecting the pulmonary artery and the aorta in the fetus that allows blood to bypass the inactive fetal lungs before birth. The failure of the duct to close at birth produces a congenital heart defect called patent ductus arteriosus. The defect mixes venous and arterial blood and overworks the heart.

ductus venosus a short blood vessel beneath the liver that allows some blood from the umbilical vein to bypass the liver and flow directly into the inferior vena cava.

Dynamic Spatial Reconstructor (DSR) a diagnostic device that uses X-rays, video equipment and computers to create a three-dimensional image of the heart or other organs.

echocardiography a noninvasive diagnostic technique that uses high-frequency sound waves to examine the structure and function of the heart.

ectopic beat a premature, usually random, heartbeat, originating from a region other than the usual pacemaker. It can result from stress, fatigue or reduced blood flow to part of the heart muscle.

electrocardiograph an instrument that records the electrical activity of the heart. The image it produces (ink curves on graph paper) is called an electrocardiogram (EKG).

embolism obstruction of a blood vessel by a blood clot or air bubble.

endocarditis an inflammation of the inner lining of the heart caused by rheumatic fever or bacterial infection.

endocardium the layer of cells that lines the inner surface of the heart.

epicardium the outer layer of the heart.

fibrillation chaotic contractions of the heart muscle, usually fatal when they occur in the ventricles.

fluoroscope a fluorescent screen that displays X-ray images of objects placed between it and a source of X-rays.

flutter rapid but orderly contractions of the heart.

foramen ovale a hole in the interatrial septum that allows blood in the fetal circulatory system to flow from the right atrium to the left bypassing the normal route of blood through the right ventricle, the pulmonary artery and the lungs.

fossa ovalis a shallow scar on the right side of the interatrial septum marking the former site of the foramen ovale.

gamma camera special camera used in nuclear scanning to count and record the emission of particles from radioactive isotopes flowing through the blood stream. Also called a scintillation camera.

heart-lung machine a device that pumps and oxygenates a patient's blood during surgery, so that the flow of blood through the patient's circulatory system bypasses the heart and lungs.

heart attack a popular term for the medical condition known as myocardial infarction.

heart block the delay or blockage of an electrical signal as it travels through the heart muscle. This delay causes the upper and lower chambers to begin contracting at different rates.

heart murmur an abnormal heart sound often caused by a defect in a heart valve. As blood flows through a narrowed or malfunctioning valve, it creates a vibration that can be heard as clearly as normal heart sounds.

hemoglobin a complex protein in red blood cells that is vital to transporting oxygen and carbon dioxide through the cardiovascular system.

high blood pressure an elevation of blood pressure, usually chronic, from unknown causes. Untreated, high blood pressure can lead to kidney failure, stroke, eye damage and heart disease.

homograft a tissue graft from any member of a species to another member of the same species.

hypertension high blood pressure. When the cause of high blood pressure cannot be traced to a particular disease or disorder, the condition is known as essential hypertension.

hypertrophy enlargement of the muscle due to thickening of muscle fibers in the heart wall. It occurs commonly in trained athletes.

inferior vena cava the large vein bringing blood from the legs and lower body to the right atrium of the heart.

intercalated disk a part of the cell membrane of a cardiac muscle fiber. Intercalated disks join adjacent cardiac muscle fibers where the fibers meet end to end.

ischemia a localized deficiency of blood caused by blockage in a blood vessel. Myocardial ischemia can cause angina pectoris or myocardial infarction.

left ventricular assist device (LVAD) any of a number of devices that pump blood from the left ventricle to the aorta to ease the workload of a damaged or diseased left ventricle.

lipids fatty substances, such as cholesterol and triglycerides, which are insoluble in water and other body fluids.

lipoproteins molecules consisting of both protein and fat, to which cholesterol attaches in order to circulate through the blood stream.

marginal artery a branch of the right coronary artery that brings blood to the right atrium and ventricle.

maximal oxygen uptake the amount of oxygen the heart and lungs can deliver to body cells during peak exercise; an index of cardiovascular fitness.

mitochondria small structures inside cells that generate energy for the normal functions of the cells.

mitral incompetence a dysfunction of the mitral valve that permits blood to flow backwards from the left ventricle to the left atrium when the ventricle contracts instead of onward to the aorta. Also known as mitral insufficiency.

mitral stenosis a narrowing of the orifice of the mitral valve. Often the result of rheumatic fever, it impedes the flow of blood through the heart and causes blood to back up in the lungs.

mitral valve the valve that connects the left atrium and left ventricle; one of the heart's two atrioventricular valves.

myocardial infarction the death of a portion of the heart muscle, usually caused by insufficient supply of oxygen to the heart due to blockage of the coronary arteries.

myocardium the thick, muscular layer of the heart wall lying between the outer and inner layers.

myofibril a minute fiber made of bundles of small filaments of protein molecules. Myofibrils run lengthwise through muscle cells.

myosin a muscle protein. Overlapping filaments of myosin and another protein, actin, inside muscle cells enable muscles to contract.

nuclear scanning a noninvasive diagnostic technique that tracks radioactive isotopes in the blood stream to produce images of the heart.

pacemaker a small cell cluster in the right atrium which emits electrical signals causing contractions of the heart. It is also known as the sinoatrial node.

pacemaker, artificial a device that electrically stimulates heartbeats.

papillary muscles small muscle columns that pull on the chordae tendineae when the ventricles contract to keep the tricuspid and mitral valves from collapsing into the atria.

pericarditis inflammation of the pericardium, the membrane surrounding the heart.

pericardium the sac that surrounds the heart.

plaques deposits of fat and other substances along the inner wall of an artery. They often grow large enough to narrow the artery opening and obstruct blood flow, as in atherosclerosis.

polyunsaturated fat a fat molecule that can accept hydrogen at more than one place on its molecular chain.

posterior descending artery a branch of the right coronary artery that brings blood down the back of the heart to both ventricles.

pulmonary circulation the circulation of blood from the heart through the lungs and back to the heart.

pulmonary artery the artery that carries blood from the right ventricle to the lungs.

pulmonary edema a condition in which the pumping ability of the left ventricle is impaired, causing fluid to accumulate in the lungs. It can result from valve disease, hypertension or coronary heart disease.

pulmonary valve the valve at the junction of the right ventricle and the pulmonary artery; one of the heart's two semilunar valves.

pulmonary veins the four veins carrying oxygenated blood from the lungs to the left atrium; the only veins in the body to carry oxygenated blood.

Purkinje fibers muscle fibers lining the walls of the lower ventricles which are thought to conduct electrical impulses causing contraction of the heart.

renin an enzyme secreted by the kidneys. Renin indirectly regulates salt metabolism and the retention of fluid.

rheumatic fever a disease that often leaves the heart valves and heart tissue inflamed. It usually occurs in childhood following a streptococcal infection.

saphenous vein one of the veins of the leg. In bypass surgery, the saphenous vein is cut from the leg and used as a graft.

sarcomere a repeating structure inside a myofibril that contains filaments of actin and myosin molecules.

saturated fats fat molecules that are chemically "filled," unable to accept more hydrogen atoms. Found mostly in foods of animal origin, they tend to raise the level of cholesterol in the blood stream.

semilunar valves the aortic and pulmonary valves, both known as semilunar valves for the crescent shape of their valve cusps.

septum a wall or partition. The two major septa of the heart are the interatrial septum and the interventricular septum.

sinoatrial (SA) node see pacemaker.

sinus a general term for a cavity, channel or depression within the body.

sinus venosus a cavity with two horns or prongs adjoining the right atrium of the embryonic heart. The right and left horns of the sinus venosus become the superior and inferior venae cavae and the coronary sinus in the mature heart.

skeleton of the heart the fibrous tissue, including the rings around the heart valves, roughly at the center of the heart.

stenosis narrowing of a valve or canal.

sternum the breastbone.

sulcus a groove or depression.

superior vena cava the major vein transporting blood from the head, arms and upper body to the right atrium of the heart.

sympatholytics drugs that influence the sympathetic nervous system, such as propranolol; used in treatment of high blood pressure.

systemic circulation the circulation of blood from the heart through the tissues of the body and back to the heart.

systole the contraction stage of the heart cycle.

tetralogy of Fallot a congenital heart abnormality consisting of four defects: a stenotic pulmonary valve, hypertrophied right ventricle, a ventricular septal defect and an aorta that overrides the septal defect and receives blood from both ventricles.

thrombosis the formation of a clot inside a blood vessel or within the chambers of the heart.

tight junctions certain points along intercalated disks where cell membranes of adjacent cardiac muscle cells fuse.

transposition of the great arteries a severe congenital heart defect in which the aorta leads from the right ventricle and the pulmonary artery from the left.

tricuspid valve the valve connecting the right atrium and right ventricle; one of the heart's two atrioventricular valves.

triglyceride a fatty substance made up of three fatty acid molecules attached to glycerol. Triglycerides are one of the body's prime energy sources.

truncus arteriosus part of the embryonic heart that leads from the right ventricle and eventually splits to form the pulmonary artery and the aorta.

Type A behavior a behavior pattern marked by competitiveness, hostility and time-urgency; believed by some heart authorities to increase the risk of coronary heart disease and heart attack.

umbilical arteries two arteries originating in the fetal pelvic region that carry blood from the fetus to the placenta.

umbilical vein the vein that carries blood from the placenta to the fetus.

vagus nerves nerves running from the brain to the abdomen which, when stimulated, slow the heart rate.

vascular system the blood vessels: veins, arteries, venules, arterioles and capillaries; excludes the heart.

vasodilators drugs that dilate peripheral blood vessels

veins blood vessels that carry blood toward the heart.

ventricles the two lower chambers of the heart. The left ventricle expels oxygenated blood to the rest of the body. The right ventricle pumps blood lacking in oxygen to the lungs.

ventricular fibrillation chaotic, ineffective beating of the ventricles, fatal unless corrected.

ventricular septal defect a congenital heart abnormality that permits blood to flow either back and forth between the ventricles or from one to the other; a hole in the interventricular septum.

venules small veins.

Illustration Credits

Index

Page numbers in bold type indicate location of illustrations.